Second Chance Reading™

Teacher Guide
for
Thrillogy

Science Fiction

Thrillogy

sundance

Sundance Publishing
234 Taylor Street
Littleton, MA 01460
800-343-8204

ISBN 0-7608-4904-8

Table of Contents

What Is Second Chance Reading?

A young child hears a story, sees her name on a gift, or sings the ABC song. Each event helps her understand more about how reading works. She uses this background when her teachers guide her through formal, sequenced tasks of learning to read. And if all goes well, this child enters fourth grade with skills and strategies that support her as the curriculum becomes more focused, more complicated, and more abstract than it was in the primary grades.

Every Kid Deserves a Second Chance

Some kids, however, make it to 4th, 7th, or even 10th grade unable to read the complex content of the upper-grade books. For whatever reason—illness, problems at home, a learning disability, a program that didn't suit the child's learning style—these kids didn't develop the most basic reading skills and strategies. We can't send them back to first grade books with giant type and tiny concepts. Just as these kids are too large for first grade desks, they are too mature for first grade readers. They need a program designed to fit their needs and their more mature sensibilities. They need structure. They need success. They need respect for who they are and what they know.

Just as these kids are too large for first grade desks, they are too mature for first grade readers.

Sundance Second Chance Reading offers upper-elementary, middle school, and high school kids a second chance to master basic reading, writing, and speaking strategies using books written for kids just like them.

- Books about the good times and bad times these kids face every day.
- Books with humor that respects the reader and makes reading fun.
- Books that look like the novels their classmates are reading.
- Books that offer hidden reading support and gradually increasing challenges without intimidating the reader.
- Books that give upper-grade kids a feeling of "I can do this!"

In other words, here is a program that uses books kids actually want to read and that supports both the teacher and the students every step of the way.

The Below-Level Readers' Great Gripe List

Just because we can't read . . .

1. People think we're dumb.
I know a whole lot about a whole lot of things—just ask me.

2. They treat us like we can't think.
I solve problems every day of the week. I just can't seem to tackle this reading thing on my own.

3. Don't think that we can't see.
Don't give me books with giant words and letters—they make me feel stupid.

4. People treat us like babies.
I don't want to read books about "Julie the Junior Reporter," . . . or "Sam the Happy Pirate." I'm not a dork; I just don't read.

5. They want us to be serious about reading all of the time.
In my neighborhood, a sense of humor can stop a problem. Can't we lighten up a little?

6. People ask us to read books they wouldn't read in a million years!
Don't give me boring books. If you think the book is boring, why would I want to read it?

7. Don't give up on us. We need practice.
Give me a book that I want to read, show me how it works, and let me practice before you listen to me read.

8. People treat us like we're the problem.
Don't give me trick questions to see if I'm trying . . . I'm not very good at this. Give me a chance.

9. People make us invisible.
Get to know us. I'm one of the most interesting kids you teach.

How Second Chance Reading Works

Sundance Second Chance Reading gives upper-elementary, middle school, and high school remedial readers the support and enjoyment they need to build the basic reading, writing, and speaking skills they might have missed the first time around.

How the Program Is Structured

Teachers work with small groups and follow a simple model: talk about the book, introduce the book, read the book, and then work on skill-building activities. Step-by-step lesson plans lead teachers and students through the guided reading process as they enjoy each new book in the *Second Chance Reading* program. The same lesson plan structure continues through each series as students work their way up through the books. This makes the program easy to manage in just a few minutes a day.

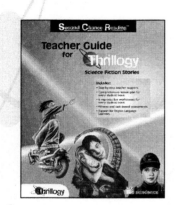

Every Second Chance Reading Teacher Guide features:

- introductory sections on the program philosophy and a complete explanation of how the program and lesson plans work.
- a step-by-step model for using *Second Chance Reading* with reluctant readers in as little as twenty minutes a day!
- a comprehensive skills chart to assist in planning and assessing students' progress.
- written and performance assessments in every lesson.
- a reproducible *Family Involvement Letter*.
- an easy-to-read answer key for every lesson.

Every Second Chance Reading Student Book features:

- gradually increasing challenges in length, language, text format, and story structure to support the reader.
- support for readers through print placement, picture-text correlation, and oral language structures.
- sophisticated humor appropriate for upper-elementary, middle school, and high school remedial readers.
- a multicultural cast of characters.

Second Chance Reading

Sparklers
Easy to read,
hard to put down
Reading Level Gr. 1–2
Interest Level Gr. 2–4
24 books, 64 pages each
850–1700+ words, 3–8 chapters

Supa Doopers—Starter Set
High-interest chapter books with
simple stories and lots of art
Reading Level Gr. 2–3
Interest Level Gr. 3–6
18 books, up to 64 pages each
1000–2850 words, 3–10 chapters

Supa Doopers—Advanced Set
Fast-paced plots with
middle school humor and art
Reading Level Gr. 2–3
Interest Level Gr. 4–8
18 books, up to 64 pages each
1100–2950 words, 3–10 chapters

Triple Play
Cliff-hanger mini-series,
unforgettable characters
Reading Level Gr. 3–4
Interest Level Gr. 4–8
4 sets of 3 books, 48 pages each
2400–3750 words, 6–8 chapters

Thrillogy
Spine-tingling tales
3 stories per book
Reading Level Gr. 4–5
Interest Level Gr. 5+
2 sets of 6 books, 48 pages each
970–2550 words/story

Fact Meets Fiction
Paired books let readers decide
which is stranger—truth or fiction
Reading Level Gr. 4–6
Interest Level 5+
4 pairs of 2 books, 96 pages each
10,000+ words, 6–8 chapters

   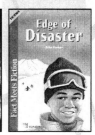

How Thrillogy Is Structured

Thrillogy offers kids all of the features that make series books so popular—characters and stories they can identify with and the look and feel of more complex novels. Each book is a mini-anthology of three stories based on one theme such as aliens, ghosts, adventure, horror, and fantasy. The series is divided into two sets, Science Fiction stories and Fantasy/Horror stories—a great introduction to genre study.

Thrillogy Student Books

Every Thrillogy Book features:
- three thrilling stories
- characters who bravely face unusual challenges
- exciting plots packed with adventures and fun
- illustrations that assist reader comprehension

Thrillogy Science-Fiction Stories

Time Zones	**Alien Invasions**	**Techno Terror**	**It Came from the Lab . . .**	**Lost in Space**	**Gadgets and Gizmos**
Stories that take you through the barriers of time.	Aliens have landed to take over Earth.	Can computers take over the world?	One thing about the future is certain. Cloning!	Meet aliens, robots, and colonists who have made space their home.	Enter the amazing world of gadgets and gizmos!

Thrillogy Fantasy/Horror Stories

 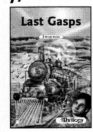    

Ghosts and Ghoulies	**Last Gasps**	**Dragon Tales**	**Terrors of Nature**	**Tales from Beyond**	**Heroic Feats**
A trio of ghost stories to set your spine shivering.	Climb aboard the ghost train for the ride of your life.	How do you deal with an angry dragon?	Plants that turn people into trees. . . a fungus that wipes out humanity.	Misplaced any friends lately? Maybe, they're trapped in an alien mine.	It's hard work being a hero.

Thrillogy
Teacher Guide

The highly structured *Second Chance Teacher Guide* provides you with the tools to meet the needs of your students and to help them progress to independent reading.

Every Teacher Guide includes:

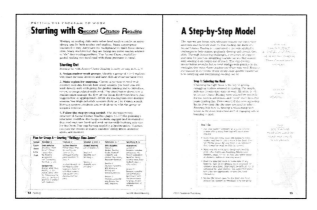

Plenty of Teacher Support
Includes sections on how to get started, managing and using the program, and how to assess below-level readers.

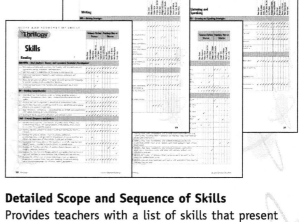

Detailed Scope and Sequence of Skills
Provides teachers with a list of skills that present a coherent, effective, and efficient program of reading and language arts instruction.

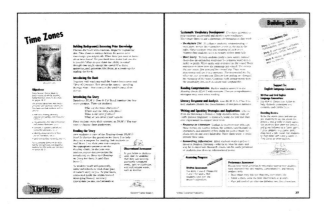

Comprehensive Lesson Plan for Every Book
Offers detailed, 2-page step-by-step plan for every student book, and activities for reading comprehension, literary analysis, listening, speaking, and writing.

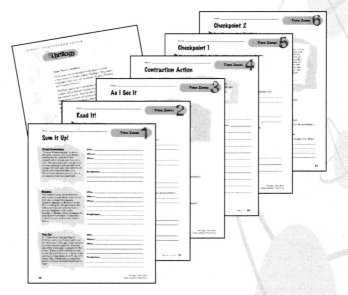

6 Reproducibles for Every Book
Includes activity sheets that reinforce reading comprehension, literary analysis, and written language skills for every student book. Also, provides a written assessment and a family letter.

How the Lesson Plans Work

Use the *Second Chance* Lesson Plans to assist in planning and conducting your guided reading lessons. Here's how the lesson plans work.

Building Background/Accessing Prior Knowledge
connect their own experiences to the book

Time Zones

Word Count: 4987

Word Count Objectives
match the book to the reader's skills

Objectives

Every *Second Chance* Reading lesson meets all of the Reading Comprehension Skills in the chart on pages 18–21.

The primary objectives met by the activities and blackline masters for this book are that students will be able to:

• read with fluency, accuracy, appropriate pacing, and intonation. (WAFSVD 1.1)

• ask questions that seek information not already discussed. (LS 1.1)

• interpret a speaker's verbal and nonverbal messages. (LS 1.2)

• identify characteristics of first-person narrative. (LRA 3.1)

• spell contractions correctly. (WOEL 1.5)

For a complete listing of all skills met by the activities and blackline masters for this book, see the chart on pages 18–21.

Building Background/Accessing Prior Knowledge

Discuss the book with students. Begin by explaining that *Time Zones* is science fiction. To access prior knowledge, you might ask: *What have you read or heard about time travel? Do you think time travel will one day be possible? How do you think the ability to travel through time might change the world?* Use these questions, and questions like these, as a warm-up for reading the book.

Introducing the Book

Together with students read the book's back cover and Table of Contents. Talk about the theme—traveling through time—that connects the book's three short stories.

Introducing the Book
looking at the book to identify the theme

Introducing the Story

Distribute *BLM 1: Sum It Up!* Read together the first story synopsis. Then ask students:

> *Who are the main characters?*
> *Where does the story take place?*
> *What is the story problem?*
> *What do you predict will happen?*

Have students write their answers on *BLM 1.* You may want to discuss their predictions.

Introducing the Story
a listening/speaking activity that builds previewing and predicting skills

Reading the Story

Give students a copy of the *Reading Guide BLM 2: Read It!* Review the questions for Story 1 to help them set a purpose for reading. Ask students to read Story 1 on their own and complete the appropriate questions on the *Reading Guide.* In the next two sessions, repeat this procedure for *Introducing the Story* and *Reading the Story* for Story 2, and then Story 3.

As students work independently, invite individuals to read aloud part of today's story to you. As you listen, assess and guide the reader toward developing fluency, accuracy, appropriate pacing, and intonation.

Observational Assessment

As you listen to students read, look for evidence that they can correctly pronounce compound words, such as *clubhouse,* and multisyllabic words, such as *familiar.*

Second Chance Reading

Thrillogy
24

Reading the Story
suggestions on how to provide guided reading support, and ways to custom-fit the lesson to readers' needs

Observational Assessment
specific oral reading, word analysis, and decoding skills to check for as students read aloud

Systematic Vocabulary Development
suggestions for strategies that develop fluency and word analysis skills

Building Skills
a whole page of activities for building vocabulary, comprehension, literary analysis, writing, speaking, listening, and decoding skills

Building Skills

Systematic Vocabulary Development Use these activities to help students understand and develop new vocabulary. Encourage them to use a dictionary or thesaurus as they work.

- *Vocabulary List* To enhance students' understanding of each story, review the vocabulary words in the list to the right. Have students write the meaning of each word. Suggest that students use a dictionary if they need help.

- *Word Study* To help students analyze new words, remind them that an unfamiliar word may be a known word with a suffix or prefix. Write *active* and *activated* on the board. Write sentences to show how the meanings are related. *The virtual dog was active. Zoe activated her virtual dog.* Then write *deactivated* and use it in a sentence. *Zoe deactivated the dog when she was done playing.* Discuss how adding *de-* changed the meaning of the word. Continue with similar words from the vocabulary list, such as *reliant* and *compatibility*.

Reading Comprehension Review student answers to the *Reading Guide BLM 2* with students. Discuss comprehension strategies they used when reading.

Literary Response and Analysis Use *BLM 3: As I See It* to help students identify the characteristics of first-person narrative.

Writing and Speaking Strategies and Applications Choose from the following activities to help students write, draw, or orally present responses to literature, using the text and their own experiences to support their work.

- *Response to Literature* Explain to students that although these stories are science fiction, the authors used humans as characters. Ask students if they think the author made the characters in one story believable. Have them write or orally present their ideas.

- *Researching Information* Have students work together to research Stephen Hawking—who he is, what he does, and why he is important. Research results can be orally presented or students may draw an informational poster.

Vocabulary List
Story 1: time capsule, vault, brawl, flabbergasted, reliant
Story 2: astronavigator, activated, compatibility, virtual, hologram
Story 3: familiar, peculiar, physicist, deja vu, theories

Support for English Language Learners

Written and Oral English Language Conventions
Use *BLM 4: Contraction Action* to help students understand and correctly spell contractions.

Decoding Review
Write the words *space* and *plunge*. Ask students to say the sound the letters *c* and *g* make in these words. Tell students that when the letters *c* and *g* are followed by *e* (*cent, gem*), *i* (*city, ginger*), or *y* (*cycle, gym*), they have a soft sound. Ask students to find other soft *c* and *g* words in *Time Zones* or other sources.

Reading Comprehension
a reminder to review Reading Guide (BLM 2) responses and discuss comprehension strategies students use

Decoding Review and Support for English Language Learners
activities that build basic skills in decoding, reading, and writing English

Literary Response and Analysis
activity (BLM 3) that explores the structural features of the book

Writing and Speaking Strategies and Applications
activities that build skills in organizing information and narrations

Assessing Progress

Written Assessment
Use *BLMs 5* and *6: Checkpoint 1* and *2* to assess that students have met the lesson's objectives.

Performance Assessment
Choose from these activities to informally observe that students have improved their oral reading, comprehension, and literary analysis skills.
- Read aloud story dialogue that they particularly like.
- Retell a story, using the book illustrations as prompts.
- Plan and conduct an interview between two story characters.

Assessing Progress
a written, reproducible test, and oral reading, comprehension, and literary analysis activities that assess all of the lesson objectives

Starting with Second Chance Reading

Working on reading skills with below-level readers can be an intimidating task for both teacher and student. Many upper-grade teachers feel they don't have the background to teach basic literacy skills. Many students feel they are facing one more teacher attempt to "fix" their reading problem. The *Second Chance* model for guided reading was developed with those pressures in mind.

Starting Out

Starting out with *Second Chance Reading* is really as easy as 1, 2, 3!

1. Assign student work groups. Identify a group of 3 to 5 students who share the same interests and have skills at about the same level.

2. Make a plan for meeting. Choose a set time to work with students each day. Decide how many sessions per week you will work directly with each group for guided reading and to introduce, review, or assign related skills work. The chart below shows how a teacher might manage the flow of one book. Each book's lesson plan suggests how to appropriately divide the reading task over multiple sessions. You might schedule sessions daily or 2 to 4 times a week. Between sessions, students can work alone or with the group on assigned activities.

3. Follow the step-by-step model. Use the step-by-step structure of *Second Chance Reading* (pages 13–17) for planning a structured workflow that keeps students engaged and motivated as they read each new book and work on the skills-building activities for that book. The step-by-step model is a flexible guide. Teachers can pace the lessons to match students' ability levels, attention spans, and interests.

Plan for Group A—Starting "Thrillogy: Time Zones"

Group	Session 1	Session 2	Sessions 3–4	Sessions 5–7	Sessions 8–10
Larry Trent Cora Josh	*Skill Building* Introduce "Time Zones". Follow Lesson Plan for *Building Background and Introducing the Book* (p. 24). *Assignments* Discuss *Word Study Activity* (p. 25). Follow Lesson Plan for *Introducing the Story* (p. 24) and do *Blackline 1* together with students.	*Guided Reading* Follow Lesson Plan for *Reading the Story* (p. 24). Introduce *Reading Guide* questions for Story 1. As students work on the *Reading Guide* questions, listen to individual students read aloud a short passage from the story.	*Guided Reading (as in Session 2)* Session 3 Students work on Story 2. Session 4 Students work on Story 3.	*Skill Building* Session 5 Review *Reading Guide*. Students complete and discuss the *Literary Response Blackline*. Session 6 Students complete and discuss a *Writing and Speaking Activity*. Session 7 Students complete and discuss the *WOEL Blackline*.	*Assessment* Session 8-9 Students complete and discuss the *Written Assessment Blacklines*. Assign practice work where students show a skills deficit. Session 10 Students complete the performance assessment tasks. Use performance to gauge student comprehension of the text.

A Step-by-Step Model

The way we use books with reluctant readers can catch their attention and motivate them to give reading one more try. *Second Chance Reading* is constructed to provide applicable challenges to help readers gradually develop and stretch their skills. Through increasing challenges, a structure of support, and time for practice, struggling readers can see that success with reading is no longer out of reach. The step-by-step model below provides below-level readers with practice in the strategies that more fluent readers use when they read. Because the student is the center of the model, kids quickly experience how satisfying and entertaining reading can be.

Step 1: Selecting the Book

Choosing the right book is the key to getting struggling readers invested in reading. Put simply, kids need books they want to read. All of the books in *Second Chance Reading* were selected by real kids for the humor, adventure, and "cool" story lines that make reading fun. Don't worry if the most appealing books don't look like the ones you read in school. Showing kids how to develop a relationship with books is the most important part of engaging kids in learning to read.

Step 1 Tips

- Use your readers' interests as a guide. Choose a book with a story line that will catch their interest.

- Know that not every book will appeal to every reader. Feel free to skip a book if the book does not fit the group. No one book is so important that it must be read for kids to succeed.

- Make sure the book suits the group's reading level. (You might use *Assessing Below-Level Readers,* pages 22–23, to help you select books at students' optimum learning level.)

- Read the selected book to make note of any features, such as vocabulary, story structure, or sentence structures, that might be difficult for, or unfamiliar to, your readers. You won't find many, but a few are appropriate to keep the book interesting.

- Review the lesson plan for the book you have selected to prepare to introduce it to the group.

When we teach SCIENCE or SOCIAL STUDIES . . . We read the chapter, then discuss what we read.

When we teach READING . . .

First, select a book that kids want to read and check it for pitfalls.

Step 2: Building Background/Accessing Prior Knowledge

Knowing something about a book makes reading easier. Giving students a chance to discuss what they know about the book's theme and to relate it to their own life gets them more interested in reading it. Listening to others discuss their experiences helps students build background that will support them as they read.

Second, warm up for reading with a discussion about how this book relates to what we already know about life.

> ### Step 2 Tips
> - Gather the group. As a warm-up activity, have a conversation with students that connects the book's main theme to their own experience.
>
> - Questions you might use are part of the *Building Background/Accessing Prior Knowledge* section of the lesson plan. Feel free to tailor these questions to the sensibilities of your readers to make the discussion more engaging.

Step 3: Introducing the Book

Book introductions motivate readers in the way that movie previews motivate viewers—readers start out already knowing something about the book. Book introductions also offer a chance to custom-fit a book to the needs of your readers and to get kids to practice the ways that good readers preview a book—by checking the covers and the Table of Contents for information.

Third, preview the book, predict what might happen in the story, and discuss special features of the book.

> ### Step 3 Tips
> - Use the *Introducing the Book and Introducing the Story* sections of the lesson plan to preview the book with students. These questions help guide students in gathering information about the setting, main characters, and story problem, and to summarize what they know before they read. A review of the *Table of Contents* draws kids further into the book by challenging them to make predictions about the story.
>
> - At this time, discuss any book features that your readers might find unfamiliar—*vocabulary, story structure,* or *sentence structure*—that you noted earlier. (See *Step 1, Selecting the Book.*)
>
> - You might also want to use the *Word Study* activity (see the *Systematic Vocabulary Development* section) to highlight vocabulary that might be unfamiliar.

Step 4: Reading the Story

To stay motivated at any task, learners need to attempt manageable chunks of work at a level they can master. The chance for students to practice reading before you listen to them and then to privately read aloud small passages for you is extremely motivating for below-level readers. *Second Chance Reading* books have been developed and leveled so that students can read successfully on their own. To enhance comprehension, each book is paired with a *Reading Guide* to help students set a purpose for reading and to focus on the most important events and ideas in that book.

Step 4 Tips

- Review the *Reading the Story* section of the lesson plan, which suggests how you might break the reading task into manageable, yet meaningful, chunks of information.

- Feel free to adjust this pacing to match the needs of your readers, knowing that the goal is for kids to read the assignment successfully.

- You might have students read the assignment before each session, for extra practice.

- Provide copies of the *Reading Guide* for students, and review the *Reading Guide* questions for that day's assignment to help students set a purpose for reading. Direct students to read the story independently and then to use the book to answer the questions on the *Reading Guide*.

- While the group is working independently, invite individual students to privately read aloud for you a section of that day's assignment. Use this opportunity to assess their progress and guide them as they read. Use the *Observational Assessment* tips in the lesson plan to help you focus your guidance and give students support as they read.

Fourth, set a purpose for reading, allow time for practice, and support learners as they tackle manageable passages on their own.

Observational Assessment

Observe for evidence that students understand punctuation. Choose a page and ask them to point out the pairs of quotation marks: *Who is speaking here? How do you know?*

Use Observational Assessment Tips to guide students as they read aloud to you.

Step 5: Building Skills

Skill-building activities that come from a reading experience are more meaningful than unrelated skills activities done separately. All of the activities provided as part of the *Building Skills* sections of the lesson plan are drawn from the vocabulary and content of the book that students have just read.

Fifth, use what we read to build new skills, matching the skills to the needs of the readers.

Step 5 Tips

- After students have read the book independently, use the lesson plan to choose the *Building Skills* activities that you have observed students need to practice.

- For some groups, you might want to take a session or two to practice every skill offered before moving on to the next book in the series.

- For other groups, you might select only one or two activities, and extend them with additional activities on the same skills as part of your whole class Language Arts program.

- You might also ask a reading resource teacher to further explore these skills with your students.

Building Skills Activities in Each Lesson Plan

Systematic Vocabulary Development activities promote word analysis skills, decoding skills, and accuracy in silent and oral reading. Below-level readers and English Language Learners need continuing practice of this kind.

Reading Comprehension is supported by the *Reading Guide*. Review and discuss the *Reading Guide* with all students after every book to gather information on how they get meaning as they read. Use your own reading strategies to offer advice, and revisit the book if necessary, to help them find answers to questions they have misinterpreted.

Literary Response and Analysis activities focus on story elements, such as setting, plot, character, and theme, and stretch a reader's flexibility in reading for different purposes. Literary analysis activities guide students to read "between the lines." Some students may need more practice in comprehension and vocabulary skills to become successful at literary analysis.

Writing and Speaking Strategies and Applications help students develop and express ideas clearly and appropriately for their audience. These activities can build communication skills at every level. English Language Learners might present information visually. Students with limited writing skills might present information orally. Students with some writing and speaking proficiency can use these activities to expand their skills.

Written and Oral English Language Conventions activities focus on spelling, punctuation, grammar, and syntax. Use these activities to review or teach basic English usage, grammar, and mechanics. These activities can help you assess students' written language strengths and deficits.

Decoding Review activities review phonics and decoding skills traditionally taught in the primary grades. They are particularly helpful for the lowest-level readers, English Language Learners, and students who need a basic review of decoding strategies.

Step 6: Assessing and Planning

Every time a student reads aloud, discusses a book, or completes a written task, teachers have an informal opportunity to assess his or her progress. Paying attention to student responses can be an invaluable source of which information about skills and strategies students use to gain and share information. Additional tasks set aside for the sole purpose of assessment help teachers confirm their observations and plan for work in future sessions.

Step 6 Tips

- Use the *Written Assessment* and *Performance Assessment* tasks provided in each lesson plan to check student progress on meeting the objectives of that lesson plan.

- You might also want to keep a copy of the *Checklist of Reading Strategies* (see page 23) for each student. Make note of the student's growing reading proficiency by checking off each strategy as you observe the student using it.

- Look over each student's work to determine where he or she might need more support. Make a few simple notes for future reference when choosing a skill focus for future lessons or for planning Language Arts activities you will review with the whole class. You might also use this information to select students to group together for similar skills practice or as a new guided reading group.

Sixth, pick a simple way to check what readers have learned and use that to decide where to go next.

Assessment Support for Every Book

Written Assessment checks student mastery of vocabulary, comprehension, literary analysis, written and oral language conventions, and decoding skills. The Written Assessment is reproducible and has been designed to test basic understanding in a minimal number of questions. For English Language Learners or students who have a writing skills deficit, you might want to present the directions and the questions orally in order to assure that the writing task itself does not mask what students actually know.

Performance Assessment provides an opportunity to assess student skill at oral and fluent reading, information retention, and literary analysis. This assessment requires almost no written response but instead provides an opportunity for students to demonstrate their current oral reading fluency and to discuss their comprehension of the book's content. Use the Performance Assessment with all students regularly in the same way you might discuss with a friend a best-seller you have just read.

Checklist of Reading Strategies provides a concise list of the basic strategies fluent readers use as they read. The checklist is reproducible and can be used to monitor student progress by checking off strategies that students currently use and helping you plan strategies to focus on in the future.

Observational Assessment offers tips to focus your guidance and support as students read aloud.

Thrillogy

Skills

Reading

	Science Fiction Stories						Fantasy/Horror Stories					
	Time Zones	Alien Invasions	Techno Terror	It Came from the Lab . . .	Lost in Space	Gadgets and Gizmos	Ghosts and Ghoulies	Last Gasps	Dragon Tales	Terrors of Nature	Tales from Beyond	Heroic Feats
WAFSVD—Word Analysis, Fluency, and Systematic Vocabulary Development												
1.1 Read aloud narrative and expository text fluently and accurately and with appropriate pacing, intonation, and expression.	✓	✓	✓	✓	✓	✓	✓	✓	✓	✓	✓	✓
1.2 Use word origins to determine the meaning of unknown words.	✓	✓	✓	✓	✓	✓	✓	✓	✓	✓	✓	✓
1.3 Understand and explain frequently used synonyms, antonyms, and homographs.					✓							
1.4 Know derived roots and affixes from Greek and Latin and use this knowledge to analyze complex words to determine meaning.					✓							
1.5 Understand and explain the figurative and metaphorical use of words in context.				✓								
RC—Reading Comprehension												
2.1 Understand how text features—such as: format, graphics, sequence, diagrams, illustrations, charts, maps—make information accessible and usable.	✓	✓	✓	✓	✓	✓	✓	✓	✓	✓	✓	✓
2.2 Analyze text that is organized in sequential or chronological order.	✓	✓	✓	✓	✓	✓	✓	✓	✓	✓	✓	✓
2.3 Discern main ideas and concepts presented in texts, identifying and assessing evidence that supports those ideas.	✓	✓	✓	✓	✓	✓	✓	✓	✓	✓	✓	✓
2.4 Draw inferences, conclusions, or generalizations about text and support them with textual evidence and prior knowledge.	✓	✓	✓	✓	✓	✓	✓	✓	✓	✓	✓	✓
2.5 Distinguish facts, supported inferences, and opinions in text.	✓	✓	✓	✓	✓	✓	✓	✓	✓	✓	✓	✓
LRA—Literary Response and Analysis												
3.1 Identify and analyze the characteristics of poetry, drama, fiction, and nonfiction and explain the appropriateness of the literary forms chosen by an author for a specific purpose.	✓	✓	✓	✓	✓	✓	✓	✓	✓	✓	✓	✓
3.2 Identify the main problem or conflict of the plot and explain how it is resolved.	✓	✓	✓	✓	✓	✓	✓	✓	✓	✓	✓	✓
3.3 Contrast the actions, motives—such as: loyalty, selfishness, conscientiousness—and appearances of characters in a work of fiction and discuss the importance of the contrasts to the plot or theme.			✓									
3.4 Understand that theme refers to the meaning or moral of a selection and identify themes—implied or directly stated—in several works.	✓	✓	✓	✓	✓	✓	✓	✓	✓	✓	✓	✓
3.5 Describe the function and effect of common literary devices—such as: imagery, metaphor, symbolism.									✓	✓		
3.6 Evaluate the meaning of archetypal patterns and symbols that are found in myth and tradition by using literature from different eras and cultures.												✓
3.7 Evaluate the author's use of various techniques—such as: appeal of characters in a picture book, logic and credibility of plot and setting, use of figurative language—to influence readers' perspectives.	✓		✓		✓		✓		✓	✓		

Thrillogy

Writing

	Science Fiction Stories						Fantasy/Horror Stories					
	Time Zones	Alien Invasions	Techno Terror	It Came from the Lab...	Lost in Space	Gadgets and Gizmos	Ghosts and Ghoulies	Last Gasps	Dragon Tales	Terrors of Nature	Tales from Beyond	Heroic Feats
WS—Writing Strategies												
1.1 Create multiple-paragraph narrative compositions: a. Establish and develop a situation or plot. b. Describe the setting. c. Present an ending.	✓	✓	✓	✓	✓	✓	✓	✓	✓	✓	✓	✓
1.2 Create multiple-paragraph expository compositions: a. Establish a topic, important ideas, or events in sequence or chronological order. b. Provide details and transitional expressions that link one paragraph to another in a clear line of thought. c. Offer a concluding paragraph that summarizes important ideas and details.		✓	✓	✓		✓	✓				✓	
1.3 Use organizational features of printed text—such as: table of contents, citations, end notes, bibliographic references—to locate relevant information.	✓	✓	✓	✓	✓	✓	✓	✓	✓	✓	✓	✓
1.4 Create simple documents by using electronic media and employing organizational features—such as: passwords, entry and pull-down menus, word searches, the thesaurus, spell checks.				✓							✓	
1.5 Use a thesaurus to identify alternative word choices and meanings.	✓	✓	✓	✓	✓	✓	✓	✓	✓	✓	✓	✓
1.6 Edit and revise manuscripts to improve the meaning and focus of writing by adding, deleting, consolidating, clarifying, and rearranging words and sentences.		✓	✓	✓	✓		✓	✓	✓	✓	✓	
WA—Writing Applications												
2.1 Write narratives: a. Establish a plot, point of view, setting, and conflict. b. Show, rather than tell, the events of the story.	✓	✓	✓	✓	✓	✓	✓	✓	✓	✓	✓	✓
2.2 Write responses to literature: a. Demonstrate an understanding of a literary work. b. Support judgments through references to the text and to prior knowledge. c. Develop interpretations that exhibit careful reading and understanding.	✓	✓	✓	✓	✓	✓	✓	✓	✓	✓	✓	✓
2.3 Write research reports about important ideas, issues, or events by using the following guidelines: a. Frame questions that direct the investigation. b. Establish a controlling idea or topic. c. Develop the topic with simple facts, details, examples, and explanations.	✓											
2.4 Write persuasive letters or compositions: a. State a clear position in support of a proposal. b. Support a position with relevant evidence. c. Follow a simple organizational pattern. d. Address reader concerns.		✓	✓	✓	✓	✓						

Thrillogy

English Language Conventions and Decoding Review

	Science Fiction Stories						Fantasy/Horror Stories					
	Time Zones	Alien Invasions	Techno Terror	It Came from the Lab…	Lost in Space	Gadgets and Gizmos	Ghosts and Ghoulies	Last Gasps	Dragon Tales	Terrors of Nature	Tales from Beyond	Heroic Feats
WOEL—Written/Oral English Language Conventions												
1.1 Identify and correctly use prepositional phrases, appositives, and independent and dependent clauses; use transitions and conjunctions to connect ideas.			✓				✓	✓	✓		✓	
1.2 Identify and correctly use verbs that are often misused—such as: lie/lay, sit/set, rise/raise—modifiers, and pronouns.					✓	✓				✓		✓
1.3 Use a colon to separate hours and minutes and to introduce a list; use quotation marks around the exact words of a speaker and titles of poems, songs, short stories, and other titles.		✓		✓								
1.4 Use correct capitalization.	✓	✓	✓	✓	✓	✓	✓	✓	✓	✓	✓	✓
1.5 Spell roots, suffixes, prefixes, contractions, and syllable constructions correctly.	✓	✓	✓	✓	✓	✓	✓	✓	✓	✓	✓	✓
DR—Decoding Review												
1.1 Identify, read, spell, comprehend, and correctly pronounce compound and two-syllable words.							✓				✓	
1.2 Identify, read, spell, comprehend, and correctly pronounce words with these consonant blends: br, cr, dr, fr, pr, tr, bl, cl, fl, pl, sl, sn, sm, st, sk, sp, sw, scr, spr, str, -ft, -lt, -nt, -st, -nk, -nd, -lk, -mp, -lf.									✓			
1.3 Identify, read, spell, comprehend, and correctly pronounce words with these consonant digraphs: -ng, sh, -sh, ch, -ch, wh, th, -th.			✓									
1.4 Identify, read, spell, comprehend, and correctly pronounce words with these less common sounds: soft g, soft c, /f/ when spelled ph or when spelled using -gh-	✓		✓						✓			
1.5 Identify, read, spell, comprehend, and correctly pronounce words with silent letters.		✓		✓								
1.6 Identify, read, spell, comprehend, and correctly pronounce words with short vowel sounds.												
1.7 Identify, read, spell, comprehend, and correctly pronounce words with long vowel sounds, including silent e spellings and alternate long vowel spellings of the long vowel sounds.												
1.8 Identify, read, spell, comprehend, and correctly pronounce words with r-controlled vowels—such as car, further—and vowel digraphs—such as cow, bread, good.									✓			✓
1.9 Identify, read, spell, comprehend, and correctly pronounce contractions, plural nouns, possessive nouns, and words with prefixes, suffixes, and inflectional endings.						✓						
1.10 Identify the number of syllables within a word and mark the word to show where the syllable breaks occur.												
1.11 Identify common slang expressions and sayings and understand their meaning and how they are used.												

Thrillogy

Listening and Speaking

	Science Fiction Stories						Fantasy/Horror Stories					
	Time Zones	Alien Invasions	Techno Terror	It Came from the Lab …	Lost in Space	Gadgets and Gizmos	Ghosts and Ghoulies	Last Gasps	Dragon Tales	Terrors of Nature	Tales from Beyond	Heroic Feats
LS—Listening and Speaking Strategies												
1.1 Ask questions that seek information not already discussed.	✓	✓	✓	✓	✓	✓	✓	✓	✓	✓	✓	✓
1.2 Interpret a speaker's verbal and nonverbal messages, purposes, and perspectives.	✓	✓	✓	✓	✓	✓	✓	✓	✓	✓	✓	✓
1.3 Make inferences or draw conclusions based on an oral report.												
1.4 Select a focus, organizational structure, and point of view for an oral presentation.	✓	✓	✓	✓	✓	✓	✓	✓	✓	✓	✓	✓
1.5 Clarify and support spoken ideas with evidence and examples.	✓	✓	✓	✓	✓	✓	✓	✓	✓	✓	✓	✓
1.6 Engage the audience with appropriate verbal cues, facial expressions, and gestures.												✓
1.7 Identify, analyze, and critique persuasive techniques—such as: promises, dares, flattery, glittering generalities; identify logical fallacies used in oral presentations and media messages.												
SA—Speaking Applications												
2.1 Deliver narrative presentations: a. Establish a situation, plot, point of view, and setting with descriptive words and phrases. b. Show, rather than tell, the listener what happens.	✓	✓	✓	✓	✓	✓	✓	✓	✓	✓	✓	✓
2.2 Deliver informative presentations about an important idea, issue, or event by the following means: a. Frame questions to direct the investigation. b. Establish a controlling idea or topic. c. Develop the topic with simple facts, details, examples, and explanations.												
2.3 Deliver oral responses to literature: a. Summarize significant events and details. b. Articulate an understanding of several ideas or images communicated by the literary work. c. Use examples or textual evidence from the work to support conclusions.	✓	✓	✓	✓	✓	✓	✓	✓	✓	✓	✓	✓

Assessing Below-Level Readers

Assessment provides teachers with the information to reinforce a student's progress in becoming a skillful reader. Teachers of below-level readers assess each student to determine a starting point for that student and to monitor progress through observation, written assessments, and interaction with students as they work.

Finding the Right Learning Level

Starting readers in the right place is critical to their success. Even a student with severe skill deficits can read simple texts. The key is to select books at the student's learning level. A learning text is one in which the student feels some challenge, can self-correct, and still demonstrates comprehension. When a student can read with 90–94% accuracy, the book is at his or her learning level.

The Five-Finger Test can be used by teachers to help older students test a new book. Ask the student to read a 100–200-word passage. Instruct him or her to raise one finger each time he or she comes to a difficult word. If the student puts up five fingers, the text is too hard.

Assessing Student Progress

Second Chance Reading provides a variety of ways to assess students as they move through the program.

The Reproducible Checklist of Reading Strategies (see page 23) sets a baseline of skills. Monitor student progress by checking off strategies that students currently use. Share the checklist with students and help them choose skills to focus on as they read independently.

Observational Assessment tips help you give students support as they read. Make a note of problem words that students encounter and incorporate them into your Language Arts lesson, Spelling lists, or Decoding reviews.

The Written Assessment is designed to test application of the basic skills for each lesson. Use student performance on the written assessment to identify skills that you will reteach before moving on or in future lessons.

The Performance Assessment tests students' oral reading fluency and comprehension of the book's content. Use the *Performance Assessment* to help you choose the *Writing and Speaking Strategies* you will focus on in future lessons.

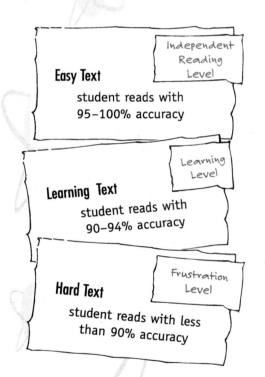

Easy Text
student reads with
95–100% accuracy

Independent Reading Level

Learning Text
student reads with
90–94% accuracy

Learning Level

Hard Text
student reads with less
than 90% accuracy

Frustration Level

Checklist of Reading Strategies

Word Level	Date
1.1 Reads simple high-frequency sight words, such as *a, the, in, on, as, to, of, for, my.*	
1.2 Understands that letters represent sounds and uses that knowledge to decode simple words. *(Can you sound the word out?)*	
1.3 Pays attention to print, noticing the features of letters and words. *(What part of the word looks like a word you already know?)*	
1.4 Uses what is known about other words to decode new words. *(What parts of this word are like other words you know?)*	
1.5 Breaks words into syllables to decode. *(What part of the word do you know?)*	
1.6 Makes a one-to-one match of spoken to written word. *(Read one word for each word you see.)*	
1.7 Searches pictures for possible word meaning. *(Does the picture give a clue about this word?)*	
1.8 Self-corrects when reading. *(Does the sentence you just read make sense in the story?)*	
Sentence Level	
2.1 Predicts what the meaning of a word might be from the surrounding text. *(What word would make sense in this sentence?)*	
2.2 Understands how punctuation affects the meaning of a sentence. *(Who is speaking? How do you know? Is this a question or a statement?)*	
2.3 Can restate a sentence in his or her own words. *(What does that sentence say?)*	
2.4 Understands and can read literary language, such as *Off the kids ran. (How might you say that if we were just talking?)*	
2.5 Distinguishes facts, supported inferences, and opinions in text. *(Based on your experience, is that true or is it the author's opinion? How could you find out?)*	
2.6 Persists in problem solving to determine meaning. *(What else might you use to try to figure out this sentence?)*	
Text Level	
3.1 Can identify main events in a story or main ideas in nonfiction.	
3.2 Can make links between personal experience and the text being read.	
3.3 Can make predictions from known events to what might happen next.	
3.4 Can identify the main problem or conflict of the plot and explain how it is resolved.	
3.5 Can identify the actions, motives, and basic traits of the main characters.	
3.6 Explores and critiques the author's message for fact, opinion, personal bias, and validity.	
Notes:	

Time Zones

Word Count: 4987

Objectives

Every *Second Chance* Reading lesson meets all of the Reading Comprehension Skills in the chart on pages 18–21.

The primary objectives met by the activities and blackline masters for this book are that students will be able to:

- read with fluency, accuracy, appropriate pacing, and intonation. (WAFSVD 1.1)

- ask questions that seek information not already discussed. (LS 1.1)

- interpret a speaker's verbal and nonverbal messages. (LS 1.2)

- identify characteristics of first-person narrative. (LRA 3.1)

- spell contractions correctly. (WOEL 1.5)

For a complete listing of all skills met by the activities and blackline masters for this book, see the chart on pages 18–21.

Building Background/Accessing Prior Knowledge

Discuss the book with students. Begin by explaining that *Time Zones* is science fiction. To access prior knowledge, you might ask: *What have you read or heard about time travel? Do you think time travel will one day be possible? How do you think the ability to travel through time might change the world?* Use these questions, and questions like these, as a warm-up for reading the book.

Introducing the Book

Together with students read the book's back cover and Table of Contents. Talk about the theme—traveling through time—that connects the book's three short stories.

Introducing the Story

Distribute *BLM 1: Sum It Up!* Read together the first story synopsis. Then ask students:

> *Who are the main characters?*
> *Where does the story take place?*
> *What is the story problem?*
> *What do you predict will happen?*

Have students write their answers on *BLM 1.* You may want to discuss their predictions.

Reading the Story

Give students a copy of the *Reading Guide BLM 2: Read It!* Review the questions for Story 1 to help them set a purpose for reading. Ask students to read Story 1 on their own and complete the appropriate questions on the *Reading Guide.* In the next two sessions, repeat this procedure for *Introducing the Story* and *Reading the Story* for Story 2, and then Story 3.

As students work independently, invite individuals to read aloud part of today's story to you. As you listen, assess and guide the reader toward developing fluency, accuracy, appropriate pacing, and intonation.

Observational Assessment

As you listen to students read, look for evidence that they can correctly pronounce compound words, such as *clubhouse,* and multisyllabic words, such as *familiar.*

Systematic Vocabulary Development
Use these activities to help students understand and develop new vocabulary. Encourage them to use a dictionary or thesaurus as they work.

- **Vocabulary List** To enhance students' understanding of each story, review the vocabulary words in the list to the right. Have students write the meaning of each word. Suggest that students use a dictionary if they need help.

- **Word Study** To help students analyze new words, remind them that an unfamiliar word may be a known word with a suffix or prefix. Write *active* and *activated* on the board. Write sentences to show how the meanings are related. *The virtual dog was active. Zoe activated her virtual dog.* Then write *deactivated* and use it in a sentence. *Zoe deactivated the dog when she was done playing.* Discuss how adding *de-* changed the meaning of the word. Continue with similar words from the vocabulary list, such as *reliant* and *compatibility*.

Reading Comprehension
Review student answers to the *Reading Guide BLM 2* with students. Discuss comprehension strategies they used when reading.

Literary Response and Analysis
Use *BLM 3: As I See It* to help students identify the characteristics of first-person narrative.

Writing and Speaking Strategies and Applications
Choose from the following activities to help students write, draw, or orally present responses to literature, using the text and their own experiences to support their work.

- **Response to Literature** Explain to students that although these stories are science fiction, the authors used humans as characters. Ask students if they think the author made the characters in one story believable. Have them write or orally present their ideas.

- **Researching Information** Have students work together to research Stephen Hawking—who he is, what he does, and why he is important. Research results can be orally presented or students may draw an informational poster.

Vocabulary List

Story 1: time capsule, vault, brawl, flabbergasted, reliant

Story 2: astronavigator, activated, compatibility, virtual, hologram

Story 3: familiar, peculiar, physicist, deja vu, theories

Support for English Language Learners

Written and Oral English Language Conventions
Use *BLM 4: Contraction Action* to help students understand and correctly spell contractions.

Decoding Review
Write the words *space* and *plunge*. Ask students to say the sound the letters *c* and *g* make in these words. Tell students that when the letters *c* and *g* are followed by *e* (*cent, gem*), *i* (*city, ginger*), or *y* (*cycle, gym*), they have a soft sound. Ask students to find other soft *c* and *g* words in *Time Zones* or other sources.

Assessing Progress

Written Assessment
Use *BLMs 5 and 6: Checkpoint 1 and 2* to assess that students have met the lesson's objectives.

Performance Assessment
Choose from these activities to informally observe that students have improved their oral reading, comprehension, and literary analysis skills.
- Read aloud story dialogue that they particularly like.
- Retell a story, using the book illustrations as prompts.
- Plan and conduct an interview between two story characters.

Name: _____

Sum It Up!

Virtual Homecoming

"Virtual Homecoming" is set in the next century. Zoe is at home, waiting for the arrival of her grandmother, whom she has never met. Her grandmother was the first woman starship pilot and left on a voyage 40 years ago. Zoe dreams of being a pilot herself some day. When Grandmother arrives, she is not exactly what Zoe expected.

Who _____

Where _____

What _____

_____

_____

Predictions _____

_____

_____

Grandma

"Grandma" is the story of Robert, who loves to read about time travel. One day, a small boy named Stephen appears at Robert's house. He is looking for his grandma, who will keep him safe until his father arrives. Stephen looks oddly familiar to Robert. Even stranger, he calls Robert's mother "Grandma." In fact, he acts as if he has visited before.

Who _____

Where _____

What _____

_____

_____

Predictions _____

_____

_____

Time Out

In "Time Out," during Tiger's birthday party, his friends gather in his clubhouse. One gift Tiger receives is a time capsule card on which he can write a message to people in the future. Tiger and his friends decide to use the card to invite a future time traveler to visit them at 6:30. At 6:30 sharp, Mrs. Gladstone, a neighbor, arrives with an unusual invitation for Tiger.

Who _____

Where _____

What _____

_____

_____

Predictions _____

_____

_____

Thrillogy: Time Zones
©2000 Sundance Publishing

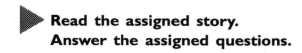
Read It!

▶ **Read the assigned story.**
Answer the assigned questions.

Time Out

1. How do the party guests plan to contact someone from the future?

_____

_____

2. Why does Mrs. Gladstone come back from the future?

_____

_____

Virtual Homecoming

3. Why does Zoe admire her grandmother?

_____

_____

4. Why don't Zoe's parents want her to be an astronavigator like her grandmother?

_____

_____

Grandma

5. What are the fuzzy waves Stephen talks about?

_____

_____

6. Why do Stephen and his father seem so familiar to Robert?

_____

_____

As I See It

Sometimes a story is told by a character in the story.
This character is a called a *first-person narrator.*
A first-person narrator uses words like
I, my, myself, me, we, us, and *our.*

The underlined words below show that the character
is a first-person narrator.

"No, listen!" I shouted. "We can make a real time machine."

My skin crawled.

▶ **Read each sentence. Underline the words that are clues to a first-person narrator. The first one is done for you.**

1. I gulped, afraid that I'd made a complete idiot of myself.

2. I almost fell over laughing.

3. We practiced writing our message on a scrap of paper.

4. "I thought you'd have intelligent machines," I said, my voice trembling.

5. I thought we could trap a time traveler.

6. Of course, I knew where they were.

7. They watched us leave as if they didn't see us.

8. I couldn't think of any way to tell my parents about what happened.

9. I knew we had a problem ahead of us.

10. My idea was that we should escape quickly.

Thrillogy: Time Zones
©2000 Sundance Publishing

Name: _____

Contraction Action

A *contraction* is the shortened form of two words.
An apostrophe is used in place of the letters
that were taken out.

The contraction <u>he'll</u> comes from the two words <u>he will</u>.

The apostrophe replaces the letters <u>wi</u> in <u>will</u>.

▶ **Read each sentence. Find the contraction. Write the two words that
the contraction comes from. The first one is done for you.**

1. "What'll we play now?" asked Kostas.   <u>What will</u>

2. "Let's pretend this computer is the Millenium Falcon."   _____

3. "Well, you think of something if you're so smart!"   _____

4. "There's no such thing, peanut brain!"   _____

5. "They'll have time machines in the future," said Tiger.   _____

6. "We didn't send it," Sanders said.   _____

7. "It doesn't matter," Tiger told him.   _____

8. "I'm afraid that I will forget him."   _____

9. "He won't remember me either."   _____

10. "It's a far different world."   _____

11. "I haven't seen him in years."   _____

12. "She'll mail the letter tomorrow."   _____

Checkpoint 1

▶ **Read each word. Write the letter of the correct meaning on the line.**

_____1. brawl   **a.** surprised or shocked

_____2. flabbergasted   **b.** like something real

_____3. activated   **c.** a fight

_____4. virtual   **d.** unproved ideas

_____5. theories   **e.** made active

▶ **Write the answer to the questions.**

6. In "Time Out," what is unusual about Tiger's neighbor, Mrs. Gladstone?

_____

_____

7. In "Virtual Homecoming," why is Zoe surprised when she first meets her grandmother?

_____

_____

▶ **Read each sentence. Underline all of the words that are clues to a first-person narrator.**

8. When we rushed out, they were nowhere to be seen.

9. The next day, I tried to tell my mother everything.

▶ **Read each sentence. On the line, write the contraction for the underlined words.**

10. What would happen if I did not mail Tiger's message? _____

11. There are not any limits on imaginary time. _____

12. Kostas is good to have around because he is big. _____

Checkpoint 2

▶ **Read this passage from "Grandma."**

* * *

The boy shook his head. "No, this is it. This is my grandma's house. Dad said I should come here fast."

"Look, kid, this can't be your grandma's. There's just Mom and me living here. No one else." Robert started to close the door.

"Robert, who is it?" His mother came out of the bathroom, drying her hair. "Who's at the door?"

"Grandma!" The child's face lit up. He rushed through the door and down the hall and grabbed her around the knees. Suddenly, he was sobbing. "The boy wouldn't let me in, and I *know* you're my grandma. Daddy said I should come to you right now! He said they're coming *now*. That's why he sent me through the fuzzy waves."

* * *

▶ **Underline the answer that correctly completes each sentence.**

1. In this passage, the boy who comes to Robert's house seems mostly

   a. content.   **c.** scared.

   b. unhurried.   **d.** silly.

2. The boy comes to Robert's house because

   a. he wanted to meet Robert.   **c.** he ran away from his father.

   b. he was bored at home.   **d.** his father told him to go to his grandma's.

▶ **Now think about the whole story "Grandma." Write the answer to this question. If you need more space, use the back of this page.**

3. If you asked the author to change one thing in this story, what would it be? Why?

   _____

   _____

   _____

   _____

Alien Invasions

Word Count: 6117

Objectives

Every *Second Chance* Reading lesson meets all of the Reading Comprehension Skills in the chart on pages 18–21.

The primary objectives met by the activities and blackline masters for this book are that students will be able to:

- read with fluency, accuracy, appropriate pacing, and intonation. (WAFSVD 1.1)

- ask questions that seek information not already discussed. (LS 1.1)

- interpret a speaker's verbal and nonverbal messages. (LS 1.2)

- identify the main problem or conflict of the plot. (LRA 3.2)

- identify and spell prefixes correctly. (WOEL 1.5)

For a complete listing of all skills met by the activities and blackline masters for this book, see the chart on pages 18–21.

Building Background/Accessing Prior Knowledge

Discuss the book with students. Begin by explaining that *Alien Invasions* is science fiction. To access prior knowledge, you might ask: *Do you think that life exists on other planets? Do you think that aliens have ever visited Earth? What do you imagine an alien might look like?* Use these questions, and questions like these, as a warm-up for reading the book.

Introducing the Book

Together with students read the book's back cover and Table of Contents. Talk about the theme—strange visitors from outer space—that connects the book's three short stories.

Introducing the Story

Distribute *BLM 1: Sum It Up!* Read together the first story synopsis. Then ask students:

> *Who are the main characters?*
> *Where does the story take place?*
> *What is the story problem?*
> *What do you predict will happen?*

Have students write their answers on *BLM 1*. You may want to discuss their predictions.

Reading the Story

Give students a copy of the *Reading Guide BLM 2: Read It!* Review the questions for Story 1 to help them set a purpose for reading. Ask students to read Story 1 on their own and complete the appropriate questions on the *Reading Guide*. In the next two sessions, repeat this procedure for *Introducing the Story* and *Reading the Story* for Story 2, and then Story 3.

As students work independently, invite individuals to read aloud part of today's story to you. As you listen, assess and guide the reader toward developing fluency, accuracy, appropriate pacing, and intonation.

Observational Assessment

As you listen to students read, look for evidence that they understand figurative language such as the simile in Story 1: *like deer in headlights.* Pause for discussion as needed.

Systematic Vocabulary Development
Use these activities to help students understand and develop new vocabulary. Encourage them to use a dictionary or thesaurus as they work.

- *Vocabulary List* To enhance students' understanding of each story, review the vocabulary words in the list to the right. Have students write the meaning of each word. Suggest that students use a dictionary if they need help.

- *Word Study* To help students analyze new words, suggest that they check to see if a word is a compound word. Have students look within long words to see if they can find short words. Demonstrate this with the word *rockfall*. Use this sentence: *People were crushed by rockfall.* First, have students identify the two words that create *rockfall*. Point out that these word parts give clues to the compound's meaning. Discuss what *rockfall* means (falling rocks). Follow a similar procedure with words such as *counterbalance* and *beaklike*.

Reading Comprehension
Review student answers to the *Reading Guide BLM 2* with students. Discuss comprehension strategies they used when reading.

Literary Response and Analysis
Use *BLM 3: What's the Problem?* to help students recognize and understand the element of conflict in a story.

Writing and Speaking Strategies and Applications
Choose from the following activities to help students write, draw, or orally present responses to literature, using the text and their own experiences to support their work.

- *Narrative* Have students imagine they were a story character. From that character's point of view, have students write their impression of an event from the story or even of another story character. Help students to improve the clarity, logic, and organization of their work.

- *Response to Literature* Have students create a book jacket that they would use for one of the stories they read. Ask students to illustrate it with an exciting or suspenseful scene.

Vocabulary List

Story 1: rockfall, counterbalance, overshooting, underbelly

Story 2: consultant, psychologist, imaginary, malfunctions

Story 3: desperate, terrified, chiming, pattering, unconscious

Support for English Language Learners

Written and Oral English Language Conventions
Use *BLM 4: Little Things Mean a Lot* with students who need more practice in identifying and spelling words with prefixes.

Decoding Review
Write the word *light* on the board and point out that the letters *gh* are silent. Ask students to find other words in the story with silent letters. Have them list the words they find.

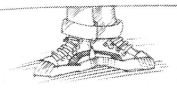

Assessing Progress

Written Assessment
Use *BLMs 5* and *6: Checkpoint 1* and *2* to assess that students have met the lesson's objectives.

Performance Assessment
Choose from these activities to informally observe that students have improved their oral reading, comprehension, and literary analysis skills.
- Read aloud a description of a character reacting to an alien.
- Create a comic strip to retell one of the stories.
- Plan and act out a newscast about a story.

Sum It Up!

The Mine

"The Mine" is about two cousins, David and Matthew. They explore a mine that closed long ago after an accident. People had seen UFOs just before the mine blew up. Odd sounds were heard at the time. The boys enter the mine. They find slime on the walls, and they, too, hear weird sounds. Something big and scary is in there with them!

Who _____

Where _____

What _____

_____

_____

Predictions _____

_____

_____

Cressy's Friend

"Cressy's Friend" is about Cressy, her dad, and her friend Frelimo. Only Cressy hears Frelimo. One day two visitors arrive at her house to study the girl. They say that she is not normal. Strange things happen during their visit. The visitors drag Cressy away to interview her, and this makes Frelimo angry.

Who _____

Where _____

What _____

_____

_____

Predictions _____

_____

_____

So Sorry!

"So Sorry!" tells the story of Katie, who leaves her house after a fight. A strange dog comes up to her on the street. She pets it and something stings her. The dog is an alien, and she has been drugged! She can't escape! She is taken to a strange house and locked in the cellar with other prisoners. She wonders what will happen to her now.

Who _____

Where _____

What _____

_____

_____

Predictions _____

_____

_____

Thrillogy: Alien Invasions
©2000 Sundance Publishing

Name: _____

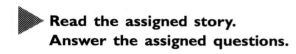

Read It!

▶ **Read the assigned story.**
Answer the assigned questions.

The Mine

1. What did David and Matthew find inside the mine?

_____

_____

2. How did Matthew's knowledge of chemistry help the boys?

_____

_____

Cressy's Friend

3. Why do two people come to Cressy's house to study her?

_____

_____

4. How do the people find out that Frelimo is real?

_____

_____

So Sorry!

5. Why do the aliens kidnap Katie and the others?

_____

_____

6. What does Katie mean when she yells, "You have stolen our lives"?

_____

_____

What's the Problem?

A *conflict* is a problem or struggle.
In many stories, there is a conflict
between two or more characters.

▶ Write a conflict for each story in the chart.
The first one is done for you.

Story Title	Characters in Conflict	Conflict
The Mine	David Matthew caterpillar-shaped alien	*David and Matthew must find a way to save themselves from a giant, alien caterpillar.*
Cressy's Friend	Cressy Frelimo Dr. Pearmain Ms. Walton	
So Sorry!	Katie dog-shaped aliens	

Thrillogy: Alien Invasions
©2000 Sundance Publishing

Little Things Mean a Lot

A *prefix* is a syllable that is added to the beginning of a word. Every prefix has a meaning.

Adding a prefix changes the meaning of a word.

The creatures <u>appeared</u> in the sky.
(meaning: *came into sight*)

The creatures <u>disappeared</u> in the sky.
(meaning: *went out of sight*)

▶ **Read each prefix and its meaning.**

> <u>dis</u> means *the opposite of*
> <u>re</u> means *again*
> <u>un</u> means *not*

▶ **Read each sentence. Circle the correct meaning of the underlined word. The first one is done for you.**

1. David does not want to <u>revisit</u> the mine.

   a. go back to   **b.** change

2. Matthew really <u>disliked</u> the smell.

   a. enjoyed   **b.** didn't care for

3. Do you think the lights will <u>reappear</u> later?

   a. be seen again   **b.** turn off

4. The boys raced over the <u>uneven</u> ground.

   a. smooth   **b.** bumpy

5. The experience with the creature was really <u>unpleasant</u>!

   a. awful   **b.** exciting

Checkpoint 1

▶ **Read each word. Write the letter of the correct meaning on the line.**

_____ 1. counterbalance

_____ 2. consultant

_____ 3. malfunctions

_____ 4. desperate

_____ 5. chiming

a. breaks down, doesn't work

b. an expert who gives advice

c. a weight that evens out an opposing weight

d. making a musical sound

e. without hope

▶ **Write the answer to the questions.**

6. In "The Mine," how do David and Matthew save themselves from the creature?

_____

_____

7. In "So Sorry!" what do the aliens want to do with Katie?

_____

_____

8. In "Cressy's Friend," what is the conflict between Cressy and Dr. Pearmain?

_____

_____

▶ **Underline the correct meaning of the word.**

9. disagree

   a. feel good about

   b. have a different opinion

10. unfinished

   a. not completed

   b. ready to go

11. reconstruct

   a. take away

   b. build again

12. distrust

   a. not believe

   b. share ideas

Thrillogy: Alien Invasions
©2000 Sundance Publishing

Name: _____

Checkpoint 2

▶ **Read this passage from "The Mine."**

Then they heard a sound behind them. It was the sound of feet, lots of feet.

They reached the house after a frantic scramble up the side of the hill. Matthew found his father's backpack and began shoving clothes into it. "As soon as it gets light tomorrow, we are out of here," he said. "It's no use leaving now. I don't want to be wandering around the hills in the dark with that thing loose."

"The creature won't leave the mine," said David. "It lives in the mine. We just annoyed it by going in."

"Did you see it?"

"No."

"It's green, and it glows, and it spits fire—and it's big. It filled up the tunnel, and the tunnel is ten feet high."

▶ **Underline the answer that correctly completes each sentence.**

1. Matthew thinks that he and David should

   a. leave the house right away.   **c.** leave after the creature leaves.

   b. leave the house the next day.   **d.** wait for their father.

2. In this passage, David thinks the creature will

   a. go away.   **c.** come to their house.

   b. change its shape.   **d.** stay in the mine.

▶ **Now think about the whole story, "The Mine." Write the answer to this question. If you need more space, use the back of this page.**

3. Which of your friends do you think would most like this story? Why?

   _____

   _____

   _____

Techno Terror

Word Count: 4891

Objectives

Every *Second Chance Reading* lesson meets all of the Reading Comprehension Skills in the chart on pages 18–21.

The primary objectives met by the activities and blackline masters for this book are that students will be able to:

- read with fluency, accuracy, appropriate pacing, and intonation. (WAFSVD 1.1)

- ask questions that seek information not already discussed. (LS 1.1)

- interpret a speaker's verbal and nonverbal messages. (LS 1.2)

- describe the actions, motives, and appearances of characters. (LRA 3.3)

- identify prepositional phrases. (WOEL 1.1)

For a complete listing of all skills met by the activities and blackline masters for this book, see the chart on pages 18–21.

Building Background/Accessing Prior Knowledge

Discuss the book with students. Begin by explaining that *Techno Terror* is science fiction. To access prior knowledge, you might ask: *Do you think life will be better or worse in the future? What will future machines be able to do? What might change as machines get smarter?* Use these questions, and questions like these, as a warm-up for reading the book.

Introducing the Book

Together with students read the book's back cover and Table of Contents. Talk about the theme—future terrors that people might face—that connects the book's three short stories.

Introducing the Story

Distribute *BLM 1: Sum It Up!* Read together the first story synopsis. Then ask students:

> *Who are the main characters?*
> *Where does the story take place?*
> *What is the story problem?*
> *What do you predict will happen?*

Have students write their answers on *BLM 1.* You may want to discuss their predictions.

Reading the Story

Give students a copy of the *Reading Guide BLM 2: Read It!* Review the questions for Story 1 to help them set a purpose for reading. Ask students to read Story 1 on their own and complete the appropriate questions on the *Reading Guide.* In the next two sessions, repeat this procedure for *Introducing the Story* and *Reading the Story* for Story 2, and then Story 3.

As students work independently, invite individuals to read aloud part of today's story to you. As you listen, assess and guide the reader toward developing fluency, accuracy, appropriate pacing, and intonation.

Observational Assessment

As you listen to students read Story 2, look for evidence that they can decode words that contain silent letters, such as the *w* in answer or the *b* in thumb.

Systematic Vocabulary Development Use these activities to help students understand and develop new vocabulary. Encourage them to use a dictionary or thesaurus as they work.

- *Vocabulary List* To enhance students' understanding of each story, review the vocabulary words in the list to the right. Have students write the meaning of each word. Suggest that students use a dictionary if they need help.

- *Word Study* Explain that science fiction often contains invented technical words. Students can often figure out the meaning of new words, by recalling known words that are similar. Point out that the words *school, scholarship, scholar,* and *scholastic* all have the same root—the Latin word *schola,* meaning "school." The word ending *-ium,* which students may know from *aquarium,* means a place where something happens. From this, students can probably infer the meaning of the word *scholarium* in the first story.

Reading Comprehension Review student answers to the *Reading Guide BLM 2* with students. Discuss comprehension strategies they used when reading.

Literary Response and Analysis Use *BLM 3: About the Character* to help students understand how authors communicate the personalities of story characters to readers.

Writing and Speaking Strategies and Applications

Choose from the following activities to help students write, draw, or orally present responses to literature, using the text and their own experiences to support their work.

- *Response to Literature* Ask students to write, draw, or orally present a possible new ending to one of the stories. Suggest that students revise and edit to improve the clarity and focus of their work.

- *Persuasive Writing* Have students write a paragraph to persuade classmates that robots will be either more helpful or more harmful to future generations.

Support for English Language Learners

Written and Oral English Language Conventions
Use *BLM 4: Above and Beyond* to help students identify prepositional phrases.

Decoding Review
Use this activity with students who need practice decoding words that begin with consonant digraphs. Say: *As you page through the book, locate and write story words you see that begin with the consonant digraphs* ch, sh, th, *and* wh. *When you are done making your list, read aloud the words to a classmate.*

Assessing Progress

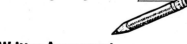

Written Assessment
Use *BLMs 5* and *6: Checkpoint 1* and *2* to assess that students have met the lesson's objectives.

Performance Assessment
Choose from these activities to informally observe that students have improved their oral reading, comprehension, and literary analysis skills.
- Read aloud scenes in which humans talk to nonhumans.
- Retell the most important story events.
- Perform a brief monologue from the point of view of a particular story character.

Sum It Up!

Rent-a-Head

"Rent-a-Head" takes place in the thirtieth century. It is told by Whitney Fran Turk, who visits the library to use a Rent-a-Head. These do the thinking for people. The girl finds herself in a future research room. A robot tells her that anyone who can't think will be phased out in the future. Since no one thinks anymore, the girl is scared.

Who _____

Where _____

What _____

_____

_____

Predictions _____

_____

_____

Ace!

"Ace!" is the story of Danny, who is destroying fighters in an arcade video game. While he's playing the game, he hears a strange voice. The voice tells him how good he is. It says that his fighter's instinct and rage could be put to better use. The voice knows Danny's darkest secrets, and Danny tries to ignore it—until something unexpected happens.

Who _____

Where _____

What _____

_____

_____

Predictions _____

_____

_____

House and Me

In "House and Me," House is a character as well as Reynard's home in the twenty-first century. House's voice soothes and relaxes the boy. Reynard thinks that machines take good care of everything. However, his parents and some other people believe that machines are taking over. When Reynard makes a decision that his parents dislike, House acts.

Who _____

Where _____

What _____

_____

_____

Predictions _____

_____

_____

Thrillogy: Techno Terror
©2000 Sundance Publishing

Read It!

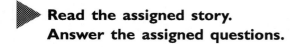

▶ **Read the assigned story.**
Answer the assigned questions.

Rent-a-Head

1. What is a Rent-a-Head?

_____

_____

2. Why does Whitney decide that it is better to use her own head?

_____

_____

Ace!

3. Why do you think Danny is so angry?

_____

_____

4. What changes when Danny becomes a real ace?

_____

_____

House and Me

5. What is House's job?

_____

_____

6. Why do Reynard and his parents disagree about House?

_____

_____

_____

Name: _____

About the Character

Sometimes authors use a character's *words*, *actions*, and *thoughts* to tell readers about the character.

"No one needs me," Danny growled.

The underlined word in the sentence tells readers that Danny is upset.

▶ **Read each sentence. Write what the underlined words tell about Danny. The first one is done for you.**

1. "Get lost!" said Danny between clenched teeth.

   Danny is angry.
   _____

2. Danny's fist came out and up fast, pulling back and letting go with a pile-driver punch.

   _____
   _____

3. Someone laughed. They're laughing at me, thought Danny.

   _____
   _____

4. When Danny saw the two cops, he ducked his head back into the hooded screen.

   _____
   _____

5. Almost instinctively, Danny's thumb twitched in the firing stud.

   _____
   _____

Thrillogy: Techno Terror
©2000 Sundance Publishing

Name: _____

Above and Beyond

A *prepositional phrase* begins with a preposition
and ends with a noun or a pronoun.

preposition   noun

The girl (in) the story is a student.

prepositional phrase

▶ **Read the prepositions in the box.**

above	before	during	on	under
below	from	over	until	among
into	through	with	after	beside

▶ **Underline the prepositional phrase in each sentence.**
Circle the preposition. The first one is done for you.

1. I walked (into) the library.

2. We saw him through the trees.

3. I stood beside a friendly robot.

4. After the talk, I went home.

5. I started doing research with him.

6. Now I know what happened during the twentieth century.

▶ **Write one sentence using two prepositional phrases. Then circle**
the prepositional phrases.

7. _____

_____

Thrillogy: Techno Terror
©2000 Sundance Publishing

J.L. Nash Jr. High Media
3100 N. Central School Rd.
Clifton, Illinois 60927

Name: _____

Checkpoint 1

▶ **Read each word. Write the letter of the correct meaning on the line.**

_____1. robotic   **a.** the act of finding fault

_____2. nebulous   **b.** collecting information

_____3. composure   **c.** machine-like

_____4. criticism   **d.** calmness of manner

_____5. researching   **e.** not clear; vague

▶ **Write the answer to the questions.**

6. In "Rent-a-Head," what does Whitney learn will happen in the future to people who don't use their own head?

_____

_____

7. In "Ace!" where do you think Danny is at the end of the story?

_____

_____

▶ **Write what the underlined words tell about Reynard in "House and Me."**

8. House soothes me, better than any parent. I am relaxed, full of hope.

_____

_____

▶ **Underline the prepositional phrase in each sentence. Circle the preposition.**

9. Danny sat inside the video arcade.

10. On the screen were several fighters.

11. She paused before the library door.

12. Reynard gave orders from his mansion.

Thrillogy: Techno Terror
©2000 Sundance Publishing

Checkpoint 2

▶ **Read this passage from "House and Me."**

We plan the new game. My house-system helps me, and Jason's helps him. If I win, my house gets an extra point with Control. I am going to make sure House and I win. Then Jason let something drop.

"Mom and Dad are gone. I monitored them talking about machines taking us over."

"Were they taken to isolation counseling?" I ask.

He nods. "House is taking care of me. It's cool."

We hang up our screens. I pick up a different wave of color. House is disturbed, and I know why. Jason's house-system should have screened out his remarks about what his parents said.

▶ **Underline the answer that correctly completes each sentence.**

1. The underlined sentence in the passage means that Jason

   a. dropped a dish.

   b. said something he shouldn't have.

   c. was Reynard's good friend.

   d. spoke in a loud voice.

2. From Jason's words, you can tell that he is

   a. worried about his parents.

   b. worried about his dog.

   c. happy with his house-system.

   d. happy that he found his book.

▶ **Now think about the whole story, "House and Me." Write the answer to this question. If you need more space, use the back of this page.**

3. Do you think this story could really happen? Why or why not? Give examples from the story to support your ideas.

   _____

   _____

   _____

   _____

It Came from the Lab . . .

Word Count: 4758

Objectives

Every *Second Chance Reading* lesson meets all of the Reading Comprehension Skills in the chart on pages 18-21.

The primary objectives met by the activities and blackline masters for this book are that students will be able to:

- read with fluency, accuracy, appropriate pacing, and intonation. (WAFSVD 1.1)

- ask questions that seek information not already discussed. (LS 1.1)

- interpret a speaker's verbal and nonverbal messages. (LS 1.2)

- understand that theme refers to the message of a book. (LRA 3.4)

- use correct capitalization with names and titles. (WOEL 1.4)

For a complete listing of all skills met by the activities and blackline masters for this book, see the chart on pages 18-21.

Building Background/Accessing Prior Knowledge

Discuss the book with students. Begin by explaining that *It Came from the Lab . . .* is science fiction. To access prior knowledge, you might ask: *What do you know about clones and cloning? What do you think people may use cloning for in the future? Who or what would you clone, if you could?* Use these questions, and questions like these, as a warm-up for reading the book.

Introducing the Book

Together with students read the book's back cover and Table of Contents. Talk about the theme—uses and misuses of cloning—that connects the book's three stories.

Introducing the Story

Distribute *BLM 1: Sum It Up!* Read together the first story synopsis. Then ask students:

> *Who are the main characters?*
> *Where does the story take place?*
> *What is the story problem?*
> *What do you predict will happen?*

Have students write their answers on *BLM 1.* You may want to discuss their predictions.

Reading the Story

Give students a copy of the *Reading Guide BLM 2: Read It!* Review the questions for Story 1 to help them set a purpose for reading. Ask students to read Story 1 on their own and complete the appropriate questions on the *Reading Guide.* In the next two sessions, repeat this procedure for *Introducing the Story* and *Reading the Story* for Story 2, and then Story 3.

As students work independently, invite individuals to read aloud part of today's story to you. As you listen, assess and guide the reader toward developing fluency, accuracy, appropriate pacing, and intonation.

Observational Assessment

As you listen to students read "Clonegirl" look for evidence that they understand the figurative and metaphorical use of words in context, such as *cutting her down to size* and *standing up for.*

Systematic Vocabulary Development Use these activities to help students understand and develop new vocabulary. Encourage them to use a dictionary or thesaurus as they work.

- *Vocabulary List* To enhance students' understanding of each story, review the vocabulary words in the list to the right. Have students write the meaning of each word. Suggest that students use a dictionary if they need help.

- *Word Study* Explain that knowing the origin or root of an unfamiliar word helps in figuring out its meaning. Help students see that they can figure out the meaning of the vocabulary words *punishable, humanoid, protesters,* and *demonstrators* if they know the meaning of the words from which they originate: *punish, human, protest,* and *demonstrate.*

Reading Comprehension Review student answers to the *Reading Guide BLM 2* with students. Discuss comprehension strategies they used when reading.

Literary Response and Analysis Use *BLM 3: Think About Theme* to help students understand what theme is.

Writing and Speaking Strategies and Applications Choose from the following activities to help students write, draw, or orally present responses to literature, using the text and their own experiences to support their work.

- *Response to Literature* Discuss with students how their ideas about cloning may or may not have changed after reading the stories in this book. Have students write, draw, or orally present their opinions about cloning related to specific story content. Work with students on how they might improve the clarity, logic, and organization of their work.

- *Persuasive Writing* Have students write or orally present recommendations that will convince another reader to select and read a story in this book. Students may want to write their recommendations using a word processing program.

Vocabulary List

Story 1: punishable, antagonize, bravado, humanoid, exorbitant

Story 2: taunt, feistiness, festered, contaminant, mutant, geneticist

Story 3: atrocious, valor, hacked, protesters, demonstrators

Support for English Language Learners

Written and Oral English Language Conventions

Use *BLM 4: A Capital Idea* to help students capitalize names and titles correctly.

Decoding Review

Explain to students that when the letter *c* is followed by *e* or *i*, it usually has the soft sound of *s*. Write *replacement, cell,* and *precise* on the chalkboard. Have students find and list other words from this book that have the soft *c* sound. Suggest that students read the words aloud.

Assessing Progress

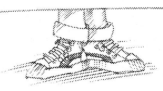

Written Assessment

Use *BLMs 5* and *6: Checkpoint 1* and *2* to assess that students have met the lesson's objectives.

Performance Assessment

Choose from these activities to informally observe that students have improved their oral reading, comprehension, and literary analysis skills.

- Read aloud a conversation between Cal and Nat, using appropriate expression.
- Retell one story as if it were being reported in a newscast.
- Conduct a panel discussion about the pros and cons of cloning.

Name: _____

Sum It Up!

Perfect Replica

"Perfect Replica" takes place in the future. Shane Maxwell and his father do not get along. Shane has decided to replace Mr. Maxwell with a humanoid—a copy that will do anything Shane wants. Shane meets with a man in a secret lab and makes all the necessary arrangements. Then, while leading his father to his fate, Shane begins to have doubts.

Who _____

Where _____

What _____

_____

_____

Predictions _____

_____

_____

Clonegirl

"Clonegirl" is the story of Natalie and her sisters, who are clones of their mother. The other girls are perfect replicas, but Natalie is not. As a result, she feels like a misfit. Then at school she meets Cal, who is blind, and they become friends. When her parents invite Cal and his parents to their home, Natalie fears that her parents' scientific experiments will ruin her new friendship.

Who _____

Where _____

What _____

_____

_____

Predictions _____

_____

_____

Just a Natural Freak

The narrator spends part of a vacation in his mother's lab. Bored, the boy cuts up different egg samples and mixes the pieces together. When protesters storm the lab, the boy and his mother leave, taking a sheep. The boy's mother finishes her cloning experiment at home, using the eggs her son had played with. The result is a mystery—except to the boy.

Who _____

Where _____

What _____

_____

_____

Predictions _____

_____

_____

Thrillogy: It Came from the Lab . . .
©2000 Sundance Publishing

Read It!

▶ **Read the assigned story.**
Answer the assigned questions.

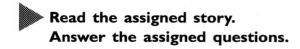

Perfect Replica

1. Why does Shane want to replace his father?

   _____

   _____

2. At the end of the story, both the man and the boy have fixed pupils.
   What conclusion can you draw?

   _____

   _____

Clonegirl

3. Why is Natalie so unhappy?

   _____

   _____

4. How might Natalie's opinion about cloning have changed at the end of the story?

   _____

   _____

Just a Natural Freak

5. What do you think the protestors would say about what the boy did?

   _____

   _____

6. What do you think about what the boy did?

   _____

   _____

Name: _____

Think About Theme

The *theme* is a message of a story or a book.

A theme of *It Came From the Lab* . . . could be that choices about cloning need to be made carefully.

▶ **Write the answer to the questions.**

1. In "Perfect Replica," why does Shane choose to clone his father?

   _____

   _____

2. How was cloning people not a good thing for Shane?

   _____

   _____

3. In "Clonegirl," why did the mother choose to clone Natalie and her sisters?

   _____

   _____

4. Why did Natalie feel it was not a good thing to be a clone?

   _____

   _____

5. In "Just a Natural Freak," why does the boy choose to mix up the eggs?

   _____

   _____

6. How was the result of his experimenting not a good thing?

   _____

   _____

7. How do you know that making careful choices about cloning is a theme of the book? Write your answer on the back of this page.

Thrillogy: It Came from the Lab . . .
©2000 Sundance Publishing

A Capital Idea

Capital letters are used for proper nouns,
names with a title, the first word in a quote,
and the pronoun *I*.

My friend Joanne visited the San Diego Zoo in California.

He saw Mrs. Wright at Dr. Morelli's office.

Then I asked, "What are you doing?"

▶ **Underline the words that should start with a capital letter.
The first one is done for you.**

1. Shane said, "my parents don't get along."

2. The man put the samples in a sealed bag labeled jackson maxwell.

3. Next year, i will work in the lab during vacation.

4. Before speaking, mr. maxwell wiped the crumbs from his lips.

5. Natsaid, "my enemy is tadman davis."

6. At recess, ms. hildegard asked nat to be the scorekeeper.

7. She asked mrs. wardell to keep an eye on me.

▶ **Write two sentences. Use a proper noun, name with a title,
words in a quote, or the pronoun *I*.**

8. _____

   _____

9. _____

   _____

Checkpoint 1

▶ **Read each word. Write the letter of the correct meaning on the line.**

_____ 1. taunt   **a.** personal bravery

_____ 2. contaminant   **b.** something produced by a major change

_____ 3. mutant   **c.** chopped

_____ 4. valor   **d.** something that spoils something else

_____ 5. hacked   **e.** an insult

▶ **Write the answer to the questions.**

6. In "Perfect Replica," what is it about Shane's father that makes Shane want to replace him?

_____

_____

7. In "Clonegirl," what might Natalie have realized about cloning after her parents made Cal new eyes?

_____

_____

8. In your own words, what is the theme of *It Came From the Lab . . .*?

_____

_____

_____

▶ **Underline the words that should start with a capital letter.**

9. Nat saw cal walking with mr. takis.

10. Shane asked the man, "what's your name?"

11. During vacation, i had to be watched by mrs. wardell.

Name: _____

Checkpoint 2

▶ **Read this passage from "Just a Natural Freak."**

Mom showed up. She was upset. "Those protesters mean business," she said. "They're going to shut us down. They have already managed to cut our power supply."

I waved at all of the equipment set out on the bench. "What about all of this stuff?"

Mom looked like she was about to cry. "It took me months and months of work to reach this stage," she wailed. "Now it'll all go down the drain."

"We could always take this stuff home," I suggested. I could hear the mob of protesters <u>charging</u> into the lobby downstairs. "Sure doesn't look like it will last long here."

"You're right," said Mom, wincing at the sound of breaking glass. "Let's do it."

▶ **Underline the answer that best completes each sentence.**

1. Mom is upset because the protesters

   a. want to start a business.

   b. threw her experiments away.

   c. cut the lab's power.

   d. want to help her.

2. In this passage, the word *charging* means that the protesters are

   a. using their credit cards.

   b. walking slowly.

   c. sitting down.

   d. rushing in.

▶ **Now think about the whole story, "It Came from the Lab . . ."**
Write the answer to this question.

3. Do you think the boy deserved to be treated like a hero at the end of the story? Why or why not?

   _____

   _____

   _____

   _____

   _____

Lost in Space

Word Count: 5004

Objectives

Every *Second Chance Reading* lesson meets all of the Reading Comprehension Skills in the chart on pages 18-21.

The primary objectives met by the activities and blackline masters for this book are that students will be able to:

- read with fluency, accuracy, appropriate pacing, and intonation. (WAFSVD 1.1)

- ask questions that seek information not already discussed. (LS 1.1)

- interpret a speaker's verbal and nonverbal messages. (LS 1.2)

- evaluate the appeal of characters. (LRA 3.7)

- use quotation marks around titles of short stories, poems, and songs. (WOEL 1.3)

For a complete listing of all skills met by the activities and blackline masters for this book, see the chart on pages 18-21.

Building Background/Accessing Prior Knowledge

Discuss the book with students. Begin by explaining that *Lost in Space* is science fiction. To access prior knowledge, you might ask: *What might the dangers be when traveling in outer space? Do you know of people who have spent time in space? How do you think this will change in the future?* Use these questions, and questions like these, as a warm-up for reading the book.

Introducing the Book

Together with students read the book's back cover and Table of Contents. Talk about the theme—life in outer space—that connects the book's three short stories.

Introducing the Story

Distribute *BLM 1: Sum It Up!* Read together the first story synopsis. Then ask students:

> *Who are the main characters?*
> *Where does the story take place?*
> *What is the story problem?*
> *What do you predict will happen?*

Have students write their answers on *BLM 1.* You may want to discuss their predictions.

Reading the Story

Give students a copy of the *Reading Guide BLM 2: Read It!* Review the questions for Story 1 to help them set a purpose for reading. Ask students to read Story 1 on their own and complete the appropriate questions on the *Reading Guide.* In the next two sessions, repeat this procedure for *Introducing the Story* and *Reading the Story* for Story 2, and then Story 3.

As students work independently, invite individuals to read aloud part of today's story to you. As you listen, assess and guide the reader toward developing fluency, accuracy, appropriate pacing, and intonation.

Observational Assessment

As you listen to students read *The Space Shed*, look for evidence that they understand frequently used homographs—words that are spelled alike, but mean different things—such as *band* and *hatch*.

Thrillogy

Systematic Vocabulary Development
Use these activities to help students understand and develop new vocabulary. Encourage them to use a dictionary or thesaurus as they work.

- *Vocabulary List* To enhance students' understanding of each story, review the vocabulary words in the list to the right. Have students write the meaning of each word. Suggest that students use a dictionary if they need help.

- *Word Study* Explain to students that many English words come from Greek and Latin. Knowing the meanings of common Greek and Latin words can make it easier to figure out what unfamiliar words mean. For example, the Latin prefix *mal-* means *bad* or *badly*; and in Greek, *micro-* means *small* and *bio-* means *life*. Help students use these prefixes to figure out the meanings of words such as *malfunction*, *micrometeoroid*, and *biosuit*.

Reading Comprehension
Review student answers to the *Reading Guide BLM 2* with students. Discuss comprehension strategies they used when reading.

Literary Response and Analysis
Use *BLM 3: Character Quiz* to help students recognize sensory details used to describe a setting.

Writing and Speaking Strategies and Applications
Choose from the following activities to help students write, draw, or orally present responses to literature, using the text and their own experiences to support their work.

- *Narrative* Have students write another ending for one of the stories in *Lost in Space*. Help students find places where they might add, delete, or consolidate ideas to improve their work.

- *Persuasive Writing* Have students write, draw, or orally present advertisements for biosuits or blasters that freeze things. The advertisements should present convincing reasons for purchasing the products.

Vocabulary List

Story 1: atmosphere, humid, fronds, scurrying, hull, module

Story 2: malfunction, disembarked, technician, sector, tradition

Story 3: adrift, biosuit, protocol, micrometeoroid, orient, velocity

Support for English Language Learners

Written and Oral English Language Conventions
Use *BLM 4: Mark Those Titles!* to help students punctuate titles of short stories, poems, and songs correctly.

Decoding Review
Write the words *write*, *debt*, *knee* and *listen* on the chalkboard. Help students to identify the silent letters in each word. Encourage them to list other words with silent letters.

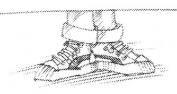

Assessing Progress

Written Assessment
Use *BLMs 5* and *6: Checkpoint 1* and *2* to assess that students have met the lesson's objectives.

Performance Assessment
Choose from these activities to informally observe that students have improved their oral reading, comprehension, and literary analysis skills.
- Read aloud, with expression, a section of exciting dialogue.
- Retell a favorite story using story illustrations as visual cues.
- Give two reasons why someone might write a story about outer space.

Name: _____

Sum It Up!

The Space Shed

When "The Space Shed" begins, Derek and Adam are battling fierce Vulags on another planet. They fight their way back to their spaceship. However, once they make it home to Earth safely, Adam acts strangely. When Derek meets his friend a few days later, he gets some bad news.

Who _____

Where _____

What _____

_____

_____

Predictions _____

_____

_____

Station Starside One

Pria lives on "Station Starside One," Earth's first space station. The station has had no contact with Earth for centuries. Then Pria discovers an abandoned machine. When she plays with the dials, she summons Jik, a technician from Earth. Jik is surprised that Pria knows almost nothing about her ancestors' planet. After he leaves, Pria decides to visit Earth.

Who _____

Where _____

What _____

_____

_____

Predictions _____

_____

_____

Adrift

In "Adrift," Uma is working outside Space Station *Plato*, where she was born and still lives. She spots a damaged spot on the hull. When the gas leak suddenly erupts, Uma loses her grip. She spins off into space and is soon beyond the reach of rescuers. Unless Uma finds a way to return to *Plato*, she will be lost in space forever.

Who _____

Where _____

What _____

_____

_____

Predictions _____

_____

_____

Thrillogy: Lost in Space
©2000 Sundance Publishing

Read It!

▶ **Read the story.**
Answer the assigned questions.

The Space Shed

1. What do you think the shed is?

_____

_____

2. What clue does the stick that Derek found at the end of the story tell you?

_____

_____

Station Starside One

3. Why does Pria know almost nothing about Earth?

_____

_____

4. Why does Pria want Jik to return to Earth?

_____

_____

Adrift

5. Why doesn't Uma want to go to Earth?

_____

_____

6. How does Uma solve her problem and get back to *Plato*?

_____

_____

Name: _____

Character Quiz

You can learn a lot about characters by what they say and do.

In *Adrift,* Uma makes many choices to get back to *Plato* safely.

Her choices tell you what kind of character she is.

▶ **Read each word. Underline 1, 2, or 3 to tell how much each word describes Uma. The first one is done for you.**

	not at all	mostly	all the time
1. helpful	1	2	3
2. brave	1	2	3
3. obedient	1	2	3
4. responsible	1	2	3
5. relaxed	1	2	3
6. smart	1	2	3

▶ **Think about Uma's character.**
Write the answer to the question.

7. Did the author make Uma a believable character? Explain your answer.

_____

_____

_____

_____

_____

Thrillogy: Lost in Space
©2000 Sundance Publishing

Mark Those Titles!

**Use *quotation marks* around the title of
short stories, poems, and songs.**

The story "The Red Planet" is about Mars.

Maria wrote a poem called "Return to Earth."

"Fly Me to the Moon" is the title of a song.

▶ **Read each sentence. Put quotation marks around each title.
The first one is done for you.**

1. "Moon Catchin' Net" is a poem by Shel Silverstein.

2. Sally Odgers is the author of Station Starside One.

3. Was the boy in The Space Shed a human or an alien?

4. The story Adrift reminds me of a poem.

5. Falling Star is the name of Sara Teasdale's poem.

6. My friend hummed a song called Take Me to Your Planet as we ate lunch.

▶ **Read the poem. Write a title to complete the sentence.
Use quotation marks.**

I dropped my tuna sandwich

And now it's floating free.

The trouble with outer-space picnics

Is the lack of gravity.

7. A title for this poem might be _____.

Checkpoint 1

▶ **Read each word. Write the letter of the correct meaning on the line.**

_____ 1. protocol   **a.** a part of an area

_____ 2. atmosphere   **b.** got out of a ship

_____ 3. sector   **c.** a detailed plan

_____ 4. adrift   **d.** the weather of a place

_____ 5. disembarked   **e.** drifting without direction

▶ **Write the answer to the questions.**

6. What might the shed be?

_____

_____

_____

7. How does Uma return to *Plato*?

_____

_____

8. Is Uma a character you admire? Why?

_____

_____

_____

▶ **Read each sentence. Put quotation marks around the title.**

9. The poem Star-Gazer is about looking at the night sky.

10. The story Journey to the Sun is a myth.

11. After I read Adrift, I wrote a song called I'll Stay Home.

Thrillogy: Lost in Space
©2000 Sundance Publishing

Checkpoint 2

▶ **Read this passage from "Adrift."**

> But even as he spoke the leak suddenly became a small volcano. Uma didn't have time to cry out as a jet of green gas shot out, hitting her helmet.
> She jerked backward automatically, realizing too late that the hull material under her left hand was giving way. Arms flailing, her helmets' visor misted over with condensation, she banged into the hull with a <u>bone-jarring crash</u>. Then she tumbled away from the station.
>
> "Uma! Uma! What's happening?"
>
> Uma didn't know. Panic rose in her throat.
>
> *Calm down!* she warned herself

▶ **Underline the answer that correctly completes each sentence.**

1. Uma is

   a. angry with her father.

   b. frightened that she is adrift.

   c. calming her father.

   d. resting from her search.

2. The phrase, <u>bone-jarring crash</u> tells you that

   a. Uma passed by the station.

   b. Uma lightly touched the station.

   c. Uma hit the station with force.

   d. Uma fell under the station.

▶ **Now think about the whole story, "Adrift." Write the answer to this question.**

3. Would you want to be with Uma in a frightening situation? Why?

   _____

   _____

   _____

   _____

   _____

Gadgets and Gizmos

Word Count: 4885

Objectives

Every *Second Chance Reading* lesson meets all of the Reading Comprehension Skills in the chart on pages 18-21.

The primary objectives met by the activities and blackline masters for this book are that students will be able to:

- read with fluency, accuracy, appropriate pacing, and intonation. (WAFSVD 1.1)

- ask questions that seek information not already discussed. (LS 1.1)

- interpret a speaker's verbal and nonverbal messages. (LS 1.2)

- identify characteristics of science fiction. (LRA 3.1)

- identify and correctly use adjectives. (WOEL 1.2)

For a complete listing of all skills met by the activities and blackline masters for this book, see the chart on pages 18-21.

Building Background/Accessing Prior Knowledge

Discuss the book with students. Begin by explaining that *Gadgets and Gizmos* is science fiction. To access prior knowledge, you might ask: *What kinds of everyday problems do machines and gadgets solve for people today? What kinds of problems might they solve for people in the future? What machines might people use in one hundred years?* Use these questions, and questions like these, as a warm-up for reading the book.

Introducing the Book

Together with students read the book's back cover and Table of Contents. Talk about the theme—present and future gadgets—that connects the book's three short stories.

Introducing the Story

Distribute *BLM 1: Sum It Up!* Read together the first story synopsis. Then ask students:

> *Who are the main characters?*
> *Where does the story take place?*
> *What is the story problem?*
> *What do you predict will happen?*

Have students write their answers on *BLM 1.* You may want to discuss their predictions.

Reading the Story

Give students a copy of the *Reading Guide BLM 2: Read It!* Review the questions for Story 1 to help them set a purpose for reading. Ask students to read Story 1 on their own and complete the appropriate questions on the *Reading Guide.* In the next two sessions, repeat this procedure for *Introducing the Story* and *Reading the Story* for Story 2, and then Story 3.

As students work independently, invite individuals to read aloud part of today's story to you. As you listen, assess and guide the reader toward developing fluency, accuracy, appropriate pacing, and intonation.

Observational Assessment

As you listen to students read, look for evidence that they use word origins to determine the meaning of unknown words, especially compound words and invented compounds, such as *headcase* and *drainhead*.

Systematic Vocabulary Development
Use these activities to help students understand and develop new vocabulary. Encourage them to use a dictionary or thesaurus as they work.

- *Vocabulary List* To enhance students' understanding of each story, review the vocabulary words in the list to the right. Have students write the meaning of each word. Suggest that students use a dictionary if they need help.

- *Word Study* Explain that the prefixes *cyber-, electro-, micro-,* and *techno-* appear often in science fiction. Although they have real meanings, in science fiction these prefixes are often added to words to make the words sound scientific. Use these examples: *cyberschool, cyberbrat, electrocyclopedia, microchip,* and *techno-trash.* Tell students that to read words with these prefixes, they should look for a familiar word within the long word.

Reading Comprehension
Review student answers to the *Reading Guide BLM 2* with students. Discuss comprehension strategies they used when reading.

Literary Response and Analysis
Use *BLM 3: Science and Fiction* to help students understand the science fiction genre.

Writing and Speaking Strategies and Applications
Choose from the following activities to help students write, draw, or orally present responses to literature, using the text and their own experiences to support their work.

- *Response to Literature* Have students write or orally present an explanation, from Tessa's point of view, about why Antina finally agreed to try the Diplomatic Hyperspace Negotiator.

- *Persuasive Writing* Have students write, draw, or orally present an advertisement that might convince others to become customers at the FIXIT shop. Ask students to critique their own work for logic and clarity.

Vocabulary List

Story 1: architect, implants, safeguards, damages

Story 2: degenerating, resolve, mediation, rationally

Story 3: catastrophe, mangled, spindly, chrome

Support for English Language Learners

Written and Oral English Language Conventions
Use *BLM 4: Big . . . Bigger . . . Biggest* to help students add *-er* or *-est* to adjectives that end with a consonant + *y.*

Decoding Review
Have students page through the book to identify the spelling and meaning of words that end with the suffix *-tion.* Ask students to locate words such as *evaporation* in which the spelling of the base word had to change.

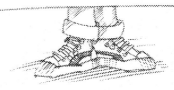

Assessing Progress

Written Assessment
Use *BLMs 5* and *6: Checkpoint 1* and *2* to assess that students have met the lesson's objectives.

Performance Assessment
Choose from these activities to informally observe that students have improved their oral reading, comprehension, and literary analysis skills.
- Read aloud one of Grixel's outbursts.
- Retell the beginning, middle, and end of one story.
- Tell why you think the author wrote "Room for Improvement."

Name: _____

Sum It Up!

Headcase

"Headcase" takes place in some future school. Dirk brags to Alistair about a schoolcase that his father invented for him. It's inside his head, and it holds all sorts of things. Alistair calls it a trick, but then finds himself trapped inside Dirk's smelly, crowded headcase. He finds that he's not alone. A classmate, Ellen, is stuck there, too.

Who _____

Where _____

What _____

_____

_____

Predictions _____

_____

_____

_____

The Diplomatic Hyperspace Negotiator

"The Diplomatic Hyperspace Negotiator" is about Grixel, a bully who torments Antina in a far-future city. Luckily, Antina's friend, Tessa, has a tool designed to solve problems without violence—a Diplomatic Hyperspace Negotiator. Now everyone waits for the results.

Who _____

Where _____

What _____

_____

_____

Predictions _____

_____

_____

_____

Room for Improvement

"Room for Improvement" is about a big problem Sarah has—Mandy Grundig. Mandy is just plain mean. She keeps taking Sarah's stuff and breaking it. Luckily, Sarah finds a new FIXIT shop. The owner not only fixes things, but also improves them. When the owner offers to fix problems as well as things, Sarah thinks of Mandy.

Who _____

Where _____

What _____

_____

_____

Predictions _____

_____

_____

_____

Thrillogy: Gadgets and Gizmos
©2000 Sundance Publishing

Name: _____

Read It!

▶ **Read the assigned story.**
Answer the assigned questions.

Headcase

1. What is it like inside Dirk's headcase?

   _____

   _____

2. Why does his dad take the headcase away?

   _____

   _____

The Diplomatic Hyperspace Negotiator

3. Why does Tessa want to use the Diplomatic Hyperspace Negotiator on Grixel?

   _____

   _____

4. What makes the ending of the story funny?

   _____

   _____

Room for Improvement

5. How does Sarah get herself in trouble with The Grunter?

   _____

   _____

6. How does Ms. Fixit help solve Sarah's problem?

   _____

   _____

Science and Fiction

***Science fiction* is a made-up story
that is based on science facts.**

Science fiction has:

• a setting in the future

• a story about space, science, or technology

• characters or machines with weird powers

▶ **Underline the sentence that has a characteristic of science fiction.
The first one is done for you.**

1. **a.** We were waiting at the hover-bus stop.

   b. The weather was cold, and I was grumpy.

2. **a.** We went out back, where we could settle this without interruption.

   b. The headcase breaks the pen down into electrical impulses
   and stores them inside.

3. **a.** Aunt Barla returned from the Andromeda system.

   b. In my dream, I lived by the ocean.

4. **a.** The laser beam transported us into the Diplomatic Hyperspace.

   b. The fireworks display included a special light show.

5. **a.** My calculator needed to be fixed after Mandy broke it.

   b. The rockets in the roller skates flew Mandy into outer space.

6. **a.** My parents should have left me on Hyperion Two.

   b. We stood staring at the stars in the sky.

Thrillogy: Gadgets and Gizmos
©2000 Sundance Publishing

Name: _____

 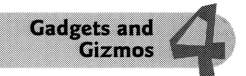

Big . . . Bigger . . . Biggest

Adjectives describe nouns or pronouns.

Jim is a big kid.

Adjectives that end in -er compare two persons, places, or things.

Jim is bigger than Tony.

Adjectives that end in -est compare three or more persons, places, or things.

Jim is the biggest kid in class.

▶ **Read each sentence. Underline the adjective that correctly completes the sentence. The first one is done for you.**

1. Dirk was _____ than a snake.

   a. skinny   **b.** skinnier   **c.** skinniest

2. Alistair is the _____ student in school.

   a. funny   **b.** funnier   **c.** funniest

3. I wake up _____ than my sister.

   a. early   **b.** earlier   **c.** earliest

4. Tech History was the _____ of all his subjects.

   a. easy   **b.** easier   **c.** easiest

5. Dirk's headcase was _____ than anyone expected.

   a. dirty   **b.** dirtier   **c.** dirtiest

6. Alistair thought it was the _____ place in the world!

   a. lonely   **b.** lonelier   **c.** loneliest

Checkpoint 1

▶ **Read each word. Write the letter of the correct meaning on the line.**

_____ 1. safeguards   **a.** a terrible disaster

_____ 2. resolve   **b.** crushed

_____ 3. catastrophe   **c.** tall and thin

_____ 4. mangled   **d.** protections

_____ 5. spindly   **e.** to find a solution to

▶ **Write the answer to the questions.**

6. In "Headcase," what did Dirk do to upset his dad?

_____

_____

_____

7. How is the Diplomatic Hyperspace Negotiator supposed to work?

_____

_____

_____

▶ **Underline the sentence(s) that have characteristics of science fiction.**

8. **a.** "What happened?" asked Antina. "Tell me what happened!"

    b. She brought back truth serum from her trip to the Andromeda System.

▶ **Underline the adjective that correctly completes the sentence.**

9. Lisa was the _____ girl in her class.

    a. lucky   **b.** luckier   **c.** luckiest

10. Tony's costume looked _____ than Tim's.

    a. scary   **b.** scarier   **c.** scariest

Name: _____

 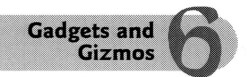

Checkpoint 2

▶ **Read this passage from "Room for Improvement."**

＊ ＊ ＊

In a daze, Sarah paid and stumbled out of the shop. She stood blinking in the sunlight, holding her new and improved skates as if they might blast off at any moment.

"Thanks. I'll just take those." The voice was snarly, mean, and it belonged to The Grunter.

"Hey!" Sarah cried. "They're mine!"

"Well, I'll just borrow them for a while. Say, five or six years," The Grunter smirked.

Sarah watched helplessly as The Grunter strapped the skates on her brawny legs. "I don't think you should do that," she began, but The Grunter cut her off.

"Too late!" she crowed, and stood up, arms waving.

＊ ＊ ＊

▶ **Underline the answer that correctly completes each sentence.**

1. The words The Grunter cut her off mean that The Grunter

   a. cut Sarah with scissors.   **c.** started talking before Sarah finished.

   b. cut in front of Sarah.   **d.** cut Sarah's hair.

2. When The Grunter says that she'll just borrow Sarah's skates, she really means

   a. to clean them.   **c.** to return them.

   b. to keep them.   **d.** to look at them.

▶ **Now think about the whole story, "Room for Improvement." Write the answer to this question. If you need more space, use the back of this page.**

3. Sarah says to Ms. Fixit, "I can handle my problems myself." If you had a problem with a bully like The Grunter, how would you handle it?

   _____

   _____

   _____

Dear Family Member:

Soon your son or daughter will begin to read a new series of books called *Thrillogy*. This series is divided into two sets of books: Science Fiction and Fantasy/Horror.

Thrillogy books have enormous appeal to older readers. They feature characters and stories kids can get excited about. Each book is a mini-anthology of three stories based on themes such as time travel, aliens, ghosts, adventure, and fantasy.

While they may not look like the books you read in school, *Thrillogy* books are **real** literature geared to grab a young person's attention and hold it. *Thrillogy* books offer readers lots of reading support yet have the look and feel of more complex novels.

Family members can help encourage kids to read. Just as you would talk about a book you're reading, ask your son or daughter to talk about the *Thrillogy* books with you. Finding a few minutes to talk about these books will show him or her that you think reading is important.

Every lifelong reader started with a good book!

Sincerely,

_____

Answer Key Sci Fi

Time Zones

1 Sum It Up! (Possible answers)
Who a boy named Tiger, his friends, Mrs. Gladstone **Where** Tiger's clubhouse
What Tiger and his friends invite a time traveler to visit them. **Predictions** Mrs. Gladstone is the time traveler.
Who Zoe, her grandmother, her parents
Where Zoe's home **What** Zoe meets her grandmother. **Predictions** She is not exciting.
Who Robert, his mother, Stephen, Stephen's father **Where** Robert's house **What** A strange child, Stephen, comes to Robert's house looking for his gramdma. **Predictions** Stephen is an alien.

2 Read It! (Possible answers)
1. They will write a message and put it into a time capsule to be read by people living in the future. 2. She comes back to find people with imagination. 3. She thinks her grandmother is beautiful and has an exciting life. 4. They know that if Zoe leaves on a starship they may never see her again. 5. a time machine that brings him back from the future 6. The father is Robert grown up, and the son looks like Robert did at the same age.

3 As I See It
1. I, I'd, myself 2. I 3. We, our 4. I, I, my 5. I, we 6. I 7. us, us 8. I, my 9. I, we, us 10. My, we

4 Contraction Action
1. What will 2. Let us 3. you are 4. There is 5. They will 6. did not 7. Does not 8. I am 9. will not 10. It is 11. have not 12. She will

5 Checkpoint 1 (Possible answers: 6 and 7)
1. c 2. a 3. e 4. b 5. d 6. She is a time traveler. 7. Her grandmother is younger than Zoe's mother. 8. we 9. I, my 10. didn't 11. aren't 12. he's

6 Checkpoint 2
1. c 2. d 3. Student answers should provide sound reasoning for their proposed change.

Alien Invasions

1 Sum It Up! (Possible answers)
Who David, Matthew **Where** an old mine
What Something scary is in the mine.
Predictions The boys will fight whatever it is and win.
Who Cressy, her dad, Frelimo, two visitors
Where Cressy's house **What** People say she is not normal. **Predictions** Frelimo will try to save her.
Who Katie, dog, other prisoners **Where** a street and a house **What** Katie is kidnapped by aliens.
Predictions She will escape and go home.

2 Read It! (Possible answers)
1. They hear noises and are chased by a fire-breathing creature. 2. He knew that a base would be a weapon against an acid. 3. They think that she is not normal because she uses calculus and does other strange things. 4. The skateboard follows the car, and at the crash they see green ooze and tentacles. 5. They want to learn about people on Earth. 6. She knows the aliens will change themselves to look like those they have kidnapped and live their lives.

3 What's the Problem?
"Cressy's Friend": Cressy has an invisible friend, but no one believes her.
"So Sorry!": Katie is kidnapped by aliens and wants to escape.

4 Little Things Mean a Lot
1. a 2. b 3. a 4. b 5. a 6. b

5 Checkpoint 1
1. c 2. b 3. a 4. e 5. d 6. They throw base fluid on it to destroy it. 7. They want to study her. 8. Cressy knows Frelimo is not imaginary; Dr. Pearmain thinks he is. 9. b 10. a 11. b 12. a

6 Checkpoint 2
1. b 2. d 3. Student answers should include specific references to story content that their friend would enjoy.

Techno Terror

1 Sum It Up! (Possible answers)
Who Whitney Fran Turk, a robot **Where** a library **What** People who can't think will be phased out, but no one thinks. **Predictions** Whitney will start to think.
Who Danny, a voice **Where** an arcade **What** Danny tries to ignore the voice. **Predictions** Something will make Danny pay attention to the voice.
Who House, Reynard **Where** the house **What** Machines are taking good care of things, but some people think machines are taking over. **Predictions** House will do something bad.

2 Read It! (Possible answers)
1. It is a brain that is wiped clean every couple of hours so that students can use it to help with their research. 2. In the future, anyone who can't use his or her head will be phased out. Also, when Whitney does her own work, she finds lots of facts that the Rent-a-Head never mentioned. 3. People say he's no good, and he thinks no one needs him. 4. He is fighting for real and not as part of a game.
5. House controls everything for the family.
6. Reynard really likes House and agrees with everything it says and does. His parents feel House is too controlling.

3 About the Character (Possible answers)
1. Danny is angry. 2. Danny has a temper.
3. Danny is concerned about what others think of him. 4. Danny is trying to hide from the police. 5. Danny is so good at playing the game that he doesn't have to think about what he's doing.

4 Above and Beyond
1. (into) the library 2. (through) the trees 3. (beside) a friendly robot 4. (After) the talk 5. (with) him
6. (during) the twentieth century 7. (Possible answer) Whitney went (through the door) and walked (into the last room.)

5 Checkpoint 1
1. c 2. e 3. d 4. a 5. b 6. She learns that in the future anyone who can't use their own head will be phased out. 7. Danny is no longer playing a game in the arcade. The game has become real. 8. Reynard is more comforted by House than by his parents.
9. (inside) the video arcade 10. (On) the screen 11. (before) the library door 12. (from) his mansion

6 Checkpoint 2
1. b 2. c 3. Answers will vary, but should include examples from the story that support the position taken by the student.

It Came from the Lab . . .

1 Sum It Up! (Possible answers)
Who Shane, Mr. Maxwell, a man **Where** a secret lab and home **What** Shane wonders if he should replace his father with a humanoid. **Predictions** He will keep his real father.
Who Natalie, her parents, her sisters, Cal **Where** school and home **What** Natalie fears her mother will ruin her new friendship. **Predictions** Natalie's mother will not ruin things.
Who a boy, his mother **Where** a lab and home **What** He mixes up eggs in a cloning lab. **Predictions** A weird animal will be cloned.

2 Read It! (Possible answers)
1. A replacement will let Shane do anything he wants and won't be annoying. 2. Shane's father arranges to have Shane replaced too, so both the man and boy are humanoids. 3. Natalie thinks her mother creates mutants and freaks through cloning. 4. She might think it is good because Cal got new eyes. 5. that it was dangerous 6. It was wrong to fool around in his mother's lab.

3 Think About Theme

1. Because his father bothers him. 2. His father replaced him. 3. Because she was too busy to have children the normal way. 4. She felt different than everyone else. 5. He's angry and bored. 6. It created a creature made of three different animals. 7. In all of the stories, something went wrong with cloning.

4 A Capital Idea (Possible answers for 8–9)

The following words should be capitalized:
1. My 2. Jackson Maxwell 3. I 4. Mr. Maxwell 5. My, Tadman Davis 6. Ms. Hildegard, Nat 7. Mrs. Wardell 8. My sister and I both had Mr. Percy in the fourth grade. 9. Mom said, "You have an appointment with Dr. Chin."

5 Checkpoint 1 (Possible answers for 6–8)

1. e 2. d 3. b 4. a 5. c 6. He always tells Shane what to do. 7. That cloning can be good for some people. 8. That cloning can be good but it has to be done carefully. 9. Cal, Mr. Takis 10. What's 11. I, Mrs. Wardell

6 Checkpoint 2

1. c 2. d 3. Answers will vary, but students' opinions should include reasons based on story content.

Lost in Space

1 Sum It Up! (Possible answers)

Who Adam, Derek, the Vulags **Where** planet of the Vulags and Adam's house **What** Derek gets some bad news. **Predictions** Adam is going away.
Who Pria, Jik, Pria's grandfather **Where** Station Starside One **What** Pria wants to visit Earth. **Predictions** She will figure out how to get there.

Who Uma **Where** Space Station *Plato* **What** Uma is adrift in space. **Predictions** Uma will figure out a way to get back.

2 Read It! (Possible answers)

1. The shed is something that takes Adam and Derek to other planets. 2. Adam and Derek really used the shed to travel in space. 3. Station Starside One lost contact with Earth before she was born. 4. Pria wants to keep contact with Earth. 5. Uma's home is on *Plato*. 6. Uma used her biosuit to point her in the right direction and slow her velocity.

3 Character Quiz (Possible answers)

1. 3 2. 3 3. 3 4. 3 5. 2 6. 3 7. Yes. Although Uma lives in space, she is brave and solves difficult problems in a believable way.

4 Mark Those Titles!

1. "Moon Catchin' Net" 2. "Station Starside One" 3. "The Space Shed" 4. "Adrift" 5. "Falling Star" 6. "Take Me to Your Planet" 7. (Possible answer) A title for this poem might be "Space Picnic."

5 Checkpoint 1 (Possible answers for 6 and 8)

1. c 2. d 3. a 4. e 5. b 6. The shed might be a way to travel to space. 7. Uma uses her biosuit to point her in the right direction. 8. Yes. I admire Uma because she was very brave in a frightening situation. 9. "Star-Gazer" 10. "Journey to the Sun" 11. "Adrift"; "I'll Stay Home"

6 Checkpoint 2

1. b 2. c 3. (Possible answer) Yes, because Uma keeps her cool under pressure in scary situations.

Gadgets and Gizmos

1 Sum It Up! (Possible answers)
Who Dirk, Alistair, Ellen **Where** a future school **What** Alistair is trapped inside Dirk's headcase. **Predictions** Alistair and Ellen will escape.
Who Grixel, Antina, Tessa **Where** a far-future city **What** Grixel is zapped to keep him from bullying. **Predictions** He will no longer be a bully.
Who Sarah, Mandy **Where** FIXIT shop **What** Mandy is mean to Sarah. **Predictions** The FIXIT shop will fix the problem.

2 Read It! (Possible answers)
1. It's dark and crowded and smelly. Occasionally, there is a burst of light. 2. Because Dirk put two people in it. 3. Because he bullies people. 4. The Virtual Mediator punches Grixel in the nose instead of working the problem out peacefully. 5. Sarah speaks without thinking and says things that make The Grunter angry. 6. She fixes Sarah's skates so that they take The Grunter away.

3 Science and Fiction
The following sentences should be underlined:
1. a 2. b 3. a 4. a 5. b 6. a

4 Big . . . Bigger . . . Biggest
1. skinnier 2. funniest 3. earlier 4. easiest 5. dirtier 6. loneliest

5 Checkpoint 1
1. d 2. e 3. a 4. b 5. c 6. He put two people in his headcase. 7. It is supposed to resolve problems peacefully by talking to people. 8. b 9. c 10. b

6 Checkpoint 2
1. c 2. b 3. Answers will vary, but students should explain in some detail.